THE CATHOLICS NEXT DOOR

THE CATHOLICS NEXT DOOR

ADVENTURES IN IMPERFECT LIVING

GREG AND JENNIFER WILLITS

SERVANT
BOOKS

PUBLISHED BY ST. ANTHONY MESSENGER PRESS
CINCINNATI, OHIO

Cover and book design by Mark Sullivan
Cover image © Ocean | Corbis

LIBRARY OF CONGRESS CATALOGING-IN-PUBLICATION DATA
Willits, Greg.
The Catholics next door : adventures in imperfect living / Greg and Jennifer Willits.
p. cm.
Includes bibliographical references (p.   ).
ISBN 978-1-61636-135-8 (alk. paper)
1. Christian life—Catholic authors. 2. Families—Religious life. I. Willits, Jennifer. II. Title.
BX2350.3.W55 2012
248.4'82—dc23
                                    2012002377

ISBN 978-1-61636-135-8

Published by Servant Books, an imprint of St. Anthony Messenger Press.
28 W. Liberty St.
Cincinnati, OH 45202
www. AmericanCatholic.org
www.ServantBooks.org

Printed in the United States of America.
Printed on acid-free paper.

12 13 14 15 16 5 4 3 2 1

To Sam, Walter, Ben, Tommy, and Lily,
and to any others that may join our family in the future.
God has given you a clear path in life.
We pray you learn how to follow it
(see Matthew 7:13–14).

contents

acknowledgments

There are far too many people for us to properly thank, but we'd be remiss not to give it a try.

First we thank our parents, Richard and Patty Willits and Hector and Gudelia Alvarez. Your nearly one hundred combined years of marriage have given us great examples and guidance for our family life.

Thanks as well to all of our colleagues and supporters and to the audiences of our various media endeavors, particularly RosaryArmy .com, NewEvangelizers.com, SQPN.com, and The Catholic Channel.

Particular thanks go to Mike and Meghan Hilleboe, Jane and Wendell Holland, Erika and Deidre Rodriguez, and Christy Johnson for loving our kids and helping watch them while we wrote this book.

Our appreciation also goes to Mike Aquilina for suggesting this book to Cynthia Cavnar, formerly with Servant Books. Thanks go to Cindy as well, and to Louise Paré and Claudia Volkman at Servant, for seeing this book through to fruition. And if not for Patrick Madrid's kicking us in the tail, you may not have had this book in your hands for another year or more.

Lastly, thanks be to the Holy Trinity and to our Blessed Mother. Since we first embarked on a journey of Catholic ministry, we've always said we'll trust God and Mary for all that we need, and they haven't let us down yet.

My first encounter with Greg and Jennifer Willits involved light-sabers. It was a warm, sunny day in Georgia, and I had just flown in from the Netherlands for the Eucharistic Congress in Atlanta. Greg and Jennifer had invited me to stay at their house. But first, I had to earn my place. Still on the front porch, one of the kids handed me a silver-colored lightsaber and gave the other Jedi weapon, red-bladed, to his father. The other kids stepped back in anticipation of the fight they clearly expected of us.

The pictures that Jennifer took that day remind me how surreal the scene must have looked to the neighbors, had they been watching: A couple of excited kids watch how their father crosses blades with this other "father," this priest in black from Holland. I rack my brain to find a fitting *Star Wars* quote for the occasion. "Your feeble skills are no match for the power of the Dutch side," I try. But it is me who is defeated. The kids cheer.

Our common fascination with *Star Wars* was just one of the many things we had talked about in the e-mails we exchanged in the months leading up to that day. We had another thing in common: We were "podcasters."

In a tiny closet, with blue walls and a small desk, surrounded by clothes and shoes, Greg and Jennifer recorded audio programs that people from all over the world could download and listen to on their iPod or computer. I was one of their listeners.

Every week, I would listen to stories about their kids, reviews of Catholic books they had read, discussions about the Rosary Army Apostolate, which they had started a few years before, or ideas about the best turkey recipe for Thanksgiving.

Funny, passionate, lively, and above all: real. Real parents. Real Catholics. Not perfect, but always open to God's grace to do better. No saints, but always sharing their desire to grow in faith and virtue. While radio and television often show us a fake and constructed version of reality, Greg and Jennifer were refreshingly honest and unscripted. What you hear is what you get.

When we handed the plastic lightsabers over to the kids and sat down at the kitchen table, we talked as if we had known each other for years—even though we had just met. Soon, sparks of creativity and enthusiasm lit up the room. Passionate about new media and evangelization, we came up with crazy ideas and ambitious plans. But none of us could have predicted what God had in store for the years that followed.

Unexpected opportunities. Difficult choices. Tough challenges as well as amazing adventures and small miracles. And at every major fork in the road, a return to prayer to provide clarity and guidance.

In his apostolic exhortation about the family, *Familiaris Consortio*, Bl. Pope John Paul II reminded families of their unique role as "witnesses of Christ 'to the end of the earth,' missionaries, in the true and proper sense, of love and life" (*Familiaris Consortio*, 54).

Over the years, Greg and Jennifer evolved from enthusiastic spare-time Catholic podcasters into full-time Catholic media professionals— "media missionaries" of love and life.

The book you are about to read will show you a glimpse of their journey so far. Actually, much more than a glimpse. This is who they really are. Their heart and soul on paper. Funny and thought-provoking, surprising and creative, brutally honest and vulnerable. A perfect guide to imperfect living.

Fr. Roderick Vonhögen
CEO, Star Quest Production Network
SQPN.com

introduction

We might be the ones known as "the Catholics next door," thanks to our radio show, but the reality is that there are over a billion others in the world who can also claim that title. The word *catholic* means "universal." To be one of "the Catholics next door" simply means to try our very best to live out our faith in the world today. This means loving God and loving our neighbor (who is really anyone we encounter in life).

Are Greg and Jennifer Willits experts at Catholic living? Hardly. But we sincerely want to be.

Are we perfect parents with the perfect Catholic family? We wish we could say we were.

Perhaps you could say the same about yourself.

At World Youth Day 2011, Archbishop Timothy Dolan of New York told those in attendance, "When we admit our faith is weak, when we admit our faith is shaky, when we admit that our faith isn't what it should be, actually we're exercising it, and we're making it more and more firm."[1]

That's a little bit of what this book is about.

This is not just a collection of anecdotes about family relationships and personal encounters with God. It's about living out our faith in today's world while constantly stumbling and pushing forward. It

---

1. Timothy Dolan, quoted by Gretchen R. Crowe in "Admit Faith Is Weak, New York Archbishop Tells Young People in Madrid," Catholic News Service, August 17, 2011.

includes just one Catholic family's example. And hopefully, through our sharing our own strivings and pitfalls, you'll discover insight into how you might have a stronger, more fruitful relationship with God while working through the imperfections of your life.

This book is simply about realizing that we're not the best Catholics that we could be but that we want to get there. It's about realizing that our friends and neighbors and coworkers are at different places in their spiritual journeys and that we're called to accompany them along the way, despite our imperfections. And more than anything, this book is simply intended to provide you with the comfort of knowing that you're not alone in your journey toward Christ.

Being one of "the Catholics next door"—whether you're a single person, a priest, a nun, a spouse, or just a kid—can be unbearably difficult in today's world. Sometimes it helps just to know that others are on the same narrow path as you and that others are stumbling just as you are. For we all stumble in our faith journey, for sure. But all of us are on a journey to a closer relationship with Christ.

And *that's* what this book is about.

It's about the path, and the potholes, and the trampolines, and the parachutes, and the fire-breathing dragons, and all of the other weirdness life has to offer. But it's also about a loving God who has given us sometimes difficult paths but also clear directions on how to follow those narrow roads on the journey.

So if you've ever struggled with your Catholicism, you're not alone. This book is for you.

If you've ever doubted the Catholic Church, if just for a moment, or ever wondered where to get some solid and reasonable answers about the unexpected surprises in life, you're not alone. This book is for you.

If you've ever simply pondered why your Catholic neighbors have so many kids and why they do the weird things they do, you're not alone. This book is for you.

If you have ever felt alone on your journey toward God or simply alone in this life, know that you're not alone. This book is for you.

And if you feel so in love with your faith that you could burst, you're not alone. This book is for you.

Thank you for joining us on this interesting, inspiring, scary, enlightening, sad, happy, joyous, and miraculous journey of being *The Catholics Next Door*.

On Being a Good Neighbor

"We are called to do what we can, within the
limitations and gifts that God has given us. We
don't have to be superheroes or super saints, but we may
have to be a little nutty. For to do the work
of Christ in today's world is going to be considered
crazy by some. So don't worry if your neighbors think
you're nuts. Most likely that means you're
on the right track."

chapter one

OUR NEIGHBORS THINK WE'RE NUTS

Who Turned Out the Lights? | *Greg*

We live in a subdivision with only fifteen homes. It's a shame that, despite the small size of our neighborhood, we don't know our neighbors better than we do. In fact, we actually have on our block neighbors we've never even met.

But what we do know of those fifteen homes in our neighborhood is that we're the only Catholics around. This seems somewhat strange. I have lived in areas of Ohio and other states where Catholicism is more prominent (though not always practiced). And Catholics make up 24 percent of the population in the United States.[2]

Because our faith is not always visible, and especially because Catholicism is often mocked and belittled, we need to remind ourselves of our responsibility to be witnesses for Christ:

> You are the light of the world. A city set on a hill cannot be hidden. Nor do men light a lamp and then put it under a bushel, but on a stand, and it gives light to all in the house. Let your light so shine before men, that they may see your good deeds and glorify your Father who is in heaven. (Matthew 5:14–16)

---

2. Pew Forum on Religion and Public Life, http://religions.pewforum.org/reports, 2007.

The idea of being a witness, a light of the world, a city set on a mountain, is a daunting one. Maybe you are an introvert, or you have had a bad experience sharing your faith, or you feel unprepared or unable to quote Scripture or find a topic in the *Catechism of the Catholic Church*. It may seem easier to avoid letting people know you're a child of God, that you're a part of this great universal Church founded by Jesus Christ himself.

Perhaps you're worried that if you share your faith, you may let God down by doing it poorly. Perhaps you think that someone else can do the job better. So you just coast along and try to stay under the radar.

Years ago, when our neighborhood was first under construction, Jennifer and I bought the very first home on the street and vowed to help create a neighborhood where people lent cups of sugar and eggs when needed, where you'd tie balloons on each other's mailboxes when a new baby was born, where you'd bring a casserole when someone was sick.

Sadly, as more than a decade has passed, these hopeful aspirations have faded. Neighbors have come and gone, and our commitment to being neighborly has often been superseded by a desire for privacy, to live and let live.

This makes it even more important for us to be aware of every situation, and to take advantage of every opportunity to be a good neighbor, to reach out in small and large ways and make a difference in the lives of others. To be a light to the world.

The great news is that it's easier to be a light than you may think. It involves being aware of others' situations and taking advantage of opportunities to be good neighbors, to reach out in small and large ways and make a difference in the lives of others. It also requires a willingness to let your neighbors think you're nuts.

A Catholic Superhero With Wonder Woman Boots | *Jennifer*
My husband was throwing underwear at my face.

I was wearing a custom-made superhero outfit, complete with flowing red cape and Wonder Woman boots. My face was stoic, since that's how superheroes look, and my hair was aptly flowing in response to a well-timed breeze. At a very visible spot in our back-yard, I followed Greg's directions and climbed to the highest rung on the ladder of our children's wooden playground set.

If this scene wasn't bizarre enough to neighbors, who by now were taking notice, Greg suddenly yelled, "Action!" turned on the video camera, and proceeded to pelt my head with our son's underwear. This went on for an uncomfortably long time, since Greg underesti-mated the challenge of successfully hitting his designated target (my face) with a floppy object (the underwear) while holding the camera steady.

On another occasion Greg made me dress up like a cave woman and run through the trees in his parents' yard. And yet another time, he thought it would be funny if I picked an imaginary booger from the nose on a bust of a politician inside our state's capitol in down-town Atlanta. All of this was caught on film and then shared on the Internet.

Sometimes we remove all doubt that we're a little peculiar.

So why did Greg have me do all those scenes? Because we've got a story to tell! We were filming *That Catholic Show*, an online series, and all the silly moments mentioned above played their roles in helping put a smile on the viewer's face while we explained our Catholic faith.

But apart from the statue of the Holy Family next to our front door, the five young kids running around our yard, the worldwide nonprofit Catholic organization we're managing, and the international Catholic radio show broadcast from a room above our garage, our neighbors still might not have a clue that we're the Catholics next door. After all, Catholicism isn't meant to be seen on a billboard as much as it is meant to be lived, experienced, and shared.

If neighbors think we're weird because we have lots of kids, are unafraid to homeschool when necessary, and work in radio ministry, then I'm glad to be like St. Paul, who said, "We are fools for Christ's sake, but you are wise in Christ" (1 Corinthians 4:10).

We didn't sign up to be praised by worldly standards but only to follow the love of our lives, Jesus Christ, and the traditions and teachings of his holy Church.

While we may take our faith seriously, we are far from saintly perfection.

Trust me, there's no levitating or bilocating going on in this house.

We do, however, love our Lord, our Blessed Mother, and our faith, and we love talking about these to anyone who will listen.

In addition to *sharing* our faith, we also seek to *listen* and to *love*. Remember the saying "Preach the gospel at all times, and when necessary use words."[3]

Once you ponder the wisdom of this statement, evangelizing people to our Catholic faith becomes easier than you might think.

For example, any time I go out in public with all five of my children in tow, I know I am silently witnessing a pro-family and pro-life message. Any time I wear a T-shirt that expresses our Christian values, I am a silent witness for the faith. Whenever I smile at a stranger, I

---

3. This quote is often attributed to St. Francis of Assisi. The thought is Franciscan in spirit, but this phrase is not in his writings or in the earliest biographies of him. In chapter 17 of his Rule of 1221, Francis told the friars not to preach unless they had received the proper permission to do so. Then he added, "Let all the brothers, however, preach by their deeds" (adapted from Friar Jack's Catechism Quiz, September 23, 2002, in "Ask a Franciscan," in *St. Anthony Messenger* magazine).

spread a bit of God's love. Anytime I pray for someone in need, answer someone's call for help, or simply offer something before I'm asked, I'm living out my Catholic faith. From the loving way I treat animals, nature, and the environment to being responsible and generous with money, the opportunities to be Catholic seem almost limitless.

Catholicism is more than a religion to which we belong. It's an action word synonymous with love and charity itself.

How do you witness your Catholic faith?

Gandhi Might Not Like Me Very Much | *Greg*

I was having lunch with a coworker years ago, feeling an incredible sense of urgency that, at that moment, I had an absolute moral responsibility to convert him before we'd finished our entrées. I was throwing his way every argument for Christ that I'd ever heard, while my coworker was completely unconvinced. He wasn't argumentative. He didn't shout me down or fight for another viewpoint. He simply didn't believe what I believed. I walked away from that lunch convinced I'd failed not only my coworker but God as well.

Years later I know that my first mistake was in thinking that I somehow held the sole responsibility for converting this person— it wouldn't be the Holy Spirit who converted him but I. That's just stupid.

My second mistake was that, other than in words, I never showed this man what it was like to be a Christian. I never asked about his family life. I never looked for opportunities to lessen his workload or to compliment him. I never reached out to help him in any practical way.

7

Mahatma Gandhi purportedly said, "I like your Christ; I do not like your Christians. Your Christians are so unlike your Christ."[4] That should shake us to the core. Are we just saying that we are Christians but not acting at all like Christ?

The reality is that we live in a complicated world. At times it may seem that everybody—family, coworkers, friends, and even strangers—wants a part of us. My frequent reaction is to put defensive walls around myself. I'm a friend from five hundred feet, a superficial friend. A superficial friend is also a superficial Christian.

Our modern secular world is built on the idea that we need to feed ourselves, serve ourselves, and give the rest of the world the leftovers.

But the Christian perspective—the one that will make your neighbors raise an eyebrow at first—is to put everyone else first.

How can we fulfill our obligations to all the people who depend on us and still have the time and energy to live the gospel in the world as Jesus called us to do?

His words are clear and unmistakable: "A new commandment I give to you, that you love one another; even as I have loved you, that you also love one another" (John 13:34).

If Jesus were saying these words to a twenty-first-century audience—and he is—he might encourage us to be a bit rebellious, to be a little nuts. Because to love others may require us to do some things that don't measure up to modern-day sensibilities.

If you want to be a Christian, you have to love, and you have to put that love into action more than you simply talk about it. Being a witness does not always mean being well-versed in the Bible. It does mean living out the lessons we're taught in Scripture.

The *Catechism of the Catholic Church* teaches, "All Christians in any

---

4. This quote is often attributed to Gandhi, but its provenance is disputed.

state or walk of life are called to the fullness of Christian life and to the perfection of charity" (*CCC*, 2013, quoting *Lumen Gentium*, 40.2).

Simply put, charity is love in action.

So how do we do this? Ultimately, how do we truly love our neighbors?

Thankfully, the Church teaches us how to use our gifts to live that loving charity. Jesus tells us to feed the hungry, give drink to the thirsty, clothe the naked, house the homeless, and visit the imprisoned and the sick (see Matthew 25:31–46). These, along with burying the dead, are the corporal works of mercy. The Church also calls us to practice the spiritual works of mercy: "Instructing, advising, consoling, comforting,…forgiving and bearing wrongs patiently" (*CCC*, 2447).

We are called to do what we can, within the limitations and gifts that God has given us. We don't have to be superheroes or super saints, but we may have to be a little nutty. For to do the work of Christ in today's world is going to be considered crazy by some.

So don't worry if your neighbors think you're nuts. Most likely that means you're on the right track.

chapter two

IMPERFECTION LEADS TO PERFECTION

Realistic Goals | *Greg*

I am prone to spending too much time playing video games. I also enjoy peanut butter, popcorn, and beer. And perhaps I drink a bit too much coffee. If given the opportunity, I'd watch hours of building shows on HGTV, but I couldn't build a bookshelf if you paid me. And if I'm to be completely honest, I'd admit I'd rather sleep an extra half hour in the morning than get right to work each day.

I can boast of many other imperfections, but I won't bore you with tales of my crooked toes, of my thinning hair—which went directly past the point of being a receding hairline and straight to no hairline—or of my physique, which somewhere along the way went from one of strength and girth to just plain old girth. These imperfections aren't the ones I worry about (too much) when I catalog my traits, nor are they the areas on which I think God wants me to focus. Yes, they bug me, of course, but deep within there's a nagging that is calling me to something deeper.

Matthew 5:48 tells us, "You, therefore, must be perfect, as your heavenly Father is perfect."

There have been many times in my life when God has shown me the perfection he calls me to. When I became a dad, I realized I could definitely grow in patience. When a friend betrayed me, I knew I needed to develop a better ability to forgive. And each and every time

God revealed the need to improve some area of my life, I've experienced some sadness and pain that God would gradually replace with contentment and some semblance of joy as his will was worked out in my life.

The imperfections in life, and our struggles to overcome them, are our road signs on the pathway to holiness and sainthood.

But to become perfect, we need God to remove the scales from our eyes so that we can more readily see the imperfections. And we have to get to a point where we accept his will, over and over again, which is much easier said than done.

The Family Drill Sergeant | *Jennifer*

Despite my best efforts at being a good mother, I still managed to harbor my fair share of character flaws. Perhaps one of my biggest flaws was my inability to make peace with what I like to refer to as the bane of my existence, dinnertime. It would cause me to unravel at the seams on a regular basis. Why? Because I had developed a serious dislike of cooking this high-pressured family meal. My self-induced stress and anxiety levels would hit the ceiling on most days.

My face would even look noticeably sterner.

So much for the June Cleaver smiles I hoped to master! Those apparently expired at approximately 4 PM on any given day.

My dialogue with the children would sound like orders being barked from a hardened drill sergeant.

"Empty the trash!"

"Wash those dishes!"

"Who threw those pillows on the floor? Pick 'em up!"

I would grow increasingly agitated as the kids grew in their hunger and frustration. To top it off, I was not able to lovingly handle the open complaining from our older boys about the meal I struggled to prepare.

"We're having what? Eh! That's disgusting!"

"But you haven't even tried it!" I'd complain back.

My patience would fly. Thus I repeatedly allowed the responsibilities of feeding my family to overwhelm me and thrust me into a sea of negativity.

It took years for me to realize that being a mother would force me to contend with two major imperfections in my character: impatience and a controlling spirit. If one of the fruits of the Holy Spirit is patience (see Galatians 5:22–23), stressful scenarios made it apparent that I had missed out on that particular harvest. My response was to try to control circumstances *my* way.

It would be awesome if all I had to do was simply pray for more patience, sit back, and receive it. But the truth is, if I went to our Lord to ask for more patience, I would most likely get more trials that would try my patience.

It would be equally tremendous if I could hand over the steering wheel of my life to God and ask him to just take over (since I apparently don't know where I'm going), but that too seems easier said than done.

In my pursuit of perfection, will I ever be able to rise above some of these flaws? I eventually learned that the answer to that simple question is yes, but only with God's daily help.

Look at it this way: Imagine your body being weak and out of shape. (For me this is easy.) Now ask God to change your current physical body and grant you a physically fit body. Did anything happen? Hardly.

No matter what potential for physical fitness our human bodies possess, it is only when we put forth some grueling effort that the changes occur. That process often hurts and takes a significant amount of time.

Similarly, all of us have the potential for increased strength of character, but only if we allow God to put us in situations that will foster its growth. And that process also hurts and takes a significant amount of time.

The *Catechism of the Catholic Church* teaches, "By living with the mind of Christ, Christians *hasten the coming of the Reign of God,* 'a kingdom of justice, love, and peace.' They do not, for all that, abandon their earthly tasks; faithful to their master, they fulfill them with uprightness, patience, and love" (*CCC,* 2046, quoting *Roman Missal,* Preface of Christ the King).

It's nice to know that these imperfections of mine don't have to become a permanent part of my life. If God can turn ordinary, manmade bread into his body, then he can certainly change this physical and spiritual weakling into a perfect child of God.

Why Parents Are Insane | *Greg*

As parents we're constantly facing scream-worthy experiences. Children fighting in the back seat. Boys who leave on the bathroom floor not only underwear but underwear rolled up into a tight little soggy knot after a loving brother dumped a glass of water on their heads. Kids who pick their noses, leaving the dried remnant on the back of your favorite couch pillow. Kids who decide for no apparent reason to hurl with full force a shoe at a brand-new television. True story.

Recently our boys decided to create their own costumes and dress up as superheroes. Not well-known superheroes, mind you, but ones of their own design. Normally this kind of cooperative behavior would be worthy of praise. Look at how well they're getting along! Look at how they're helping each other toward a common goal! Our children will surely grow up to be model citizens!

Then, as our son Tommy walked through the room, I noticed he was wearing his shirt backward. Why was it backward? Well, the front of the shirt already had something on it, so Tommy had decided to show his innovative spirit all over the clear area on the back of the shirt—in permanent marker, of course. Now again, this should be no big deal. But then his brother Ben pointed out that the shirt Tom used was actually one of Ben's favorites, one we'd just brought back for him from Rome.

No matter how many years we get under our parenting belts, it's very likely that our kids will continue giving us scream-worthy experiences. In fact, we're convinced that we still make our own parents scream in exasperation, even though we've been out from under the shelter of their loving care for more than half our lives. When we got new cellphones three years in a row, for example, one of our parents was surely banging his head somewhere and muttering, "Are they even *trying* to save for retirement?"

Not only do our kids do things that make no sense and do we do things that make no sense to our parents, but it's even more likely—if not an outright certainty of human nature—that we make God shake his celestial head every single day of our lives.

The things our kids do that shake us to our core—intentionally or biologically—are often the very things we do over and over again. These are the little nitpicky things as well as the big things that we know we shouldn't do, that we know disappoint God our Father, that eventually disappoint us.

We swear when we get irritable. We watch movies that cross the line of moral acceptability. We scream at our kids when we get impatient. By splurging on ourselves instead of on others, we take advantage of the generosity God has shown us.

In essence, we do to God what our kids do to us. We put all the focus on ourselves, forgetting that if we focus on what God wants instead, our lives are much easier. And then, like our children, we expect God to clean up the mess.

A Spiritual Tornado Drill | *Jennifer*

Psalm 127:3 is perhaps one of the most perplexing passages in the Bible:

> Children too are a gift from the LORD,
> the fruit of the womb, a reward.

I occasionally like to call to mind that verse of Scripture, particularly on days when I wonder if God has a returns department for his gifts.

But one benefit of these "gifts" from God is how they regularly drive me to my knees in prayer. They remind me quite easily that all by myself I am too weak for the job of mom. I need supernatural fuel in my tank to help me survive in this loud and rambunctious home. Fuel I need, and fuel I do receive whenever I ask for it in prayer.

One afternoon I was having a stressful time with our kids. The boys were subjecting me to an unusually high volume of unruly behavior. Given how loud they normally are, let me just emphasize the unusual quality of their loudness that day. None of them were angry; they were just having a great time testing out the maximum power of their God-given vocal cords.

After an hour of this excruciating environment, my patience left me. I was tried to the point that I feared a mini-breakdown. But even in that dark emotional moment, I experienced some spiritual clarity. Rather than react harshly to the children in an effort to put an end to my suffering, I crumpled to my knees and curled up like a child in a grade-school tornado drill. I did this right in front of the children.

Once in this turtle (some might say "fetal") position, I began uttering an unbroken stream of Hail Marys. I was immovable. Locked in prayer, I was not going to emerge from my shell until I had patience and peace restored to my soul. It did not matter how long it was going to take me. I was in it for the long haul.

Thank goodness our toddler did not take advantage of that moment to climb on my back for a horsey ride!

Something else happened.

The loud and rambunctious behavior stopped, as curiosity drew the boys to wonder what had just happened to their mommy. In the next moment I felt the unmistakable hand of that toddler caressing my back.

Soon all the boys were near me, telling me it was going to be OK. They recognized what I was doing. They had heard those words of prayer in the family rosary.

They knew I was "leaning" on God, and they actually cared.

Before long I felt peace again and was able to return to my senses. I could reassure the children that all was well. Indeed, it was.

I'm a Screwup, and You Can Be One, Too! | *Greg*

A fact of our human nature is that we are flawed and directed to sinful behavior, while simultaneously being called to holiness.

On our own, holiness is unobtainable.

We are imperfect.

Only God can fix that. And more important, God *wants* to fix it.

When we acknowledge that, we can truly begin down the path of letting God, like a gentle surgeon, remove those imperfections.

We are dependent on the grace of God to strengthen us to overcome the messes we create in our lives as well as the messes others leave for us to clean up.

If you're trying to stop sinful behavior, you simply cannot do it on your own. If you blow your top at your kids, as I too often do, and you sincerely want more patience, you won't become more patient on your own. You are incapable, but God is not.

In a way it helps to know we're not the only screwups in this world. I suspect that many of the seemingly perfect parents sitting in the pew ahead of us at church, the ones with the angelic children, are screwups as well. I don't know why that helps me, but it does.

It's good to remind ourselves, especially when we're ready to throttle a kid who just spray-painted a brand new set of golf clubs, that you were a screwup before your kid was. And you still are. But you're getting better, with the help of God.

Children, those gifts from God, help us realize our dependence on God as does nothing else we experience in life. And that is one reason why they are such gifts: They remind us of our need for our heavenly Father.

It's a Family Affair

"Our family's spirituality is a work in progress. There will be victories and head-smacking

embarrassments. But as long as we maintain our

focus on Christ, stay close to him in the

sacraments, and remain loyal to the teachings of our faith

to the best of our abilities,

we will be equipped to handle any challenge God

wants to put before us. Do we pray perfectly

every day as a family? No. Do we try our best?

Yes."

chapter three

GOD'S IN THE HALLWAY, AND HE CAN HEAR THROUGH THE DOOR

An Asterisk | *Greg*

Before we get started on perhaps one of the most contentious among Catholic topics, let me point out that when Jennifer and I first got married, we weren't sure we even wanted children. She wasn't Catholic then, and I was doing a lousy job living out my faith. And the desire for offspring was just not there.

Now we have five.

God has a sense of humor. And he knows what he's doing.

Something to keep in mind.

What Do You Mean, I'm Not Done? | *Jennifer*

According to the 2001 U.S. census, the average number of family members under the age of eighteen in a household was 1.91. That's right, 1.91—slightly less than two whole children.[5]

More recently a *USA Today* analysis of the 2010 census showed that the share of the population under age eighteen has dropped in 95 percent of U.S. counties since 2000. From that we can calculate that there are now more U.S. households with dogs (forty-three million) than with children![6]

---

5. Table HH-6, "Average Population Per Household Family, 1940 to Present," U.S. Census Bureau, September 15, 2004, http://tunyurl.com/household-us-census-bureau.
6. Haya El Nasser and Paul Overberg, "Census Reveals Plummeting U.S. Birthrates," *USA Today*, June 2, 2011.

Most of society sees contraception as a guarantee of the freedom to have unlimited intimate relations with no unwanted consequences, such as a new human life being conceived. Society would have us believe that pursuing the pleasures of sexual intimacy with proper contraception is responsible behavior. Some people believe this out of pure ignorance, and others choose to believe this out of pride. What's sad to me is the alarming number of professed Catholics who practice and even advocate contraception. In fact, in a September 2005 online survey of 2,242 U.S. adults, Harris Interactive found that 90 percent of Catholics supported the use of contraception.[7]

In 2001, I could say that Greg and I exceeded the national average number of children, because we actually had two biological sons of our own. Our family was a nice even number—two adults and two children. I remember holding our second son more often than I did our first son, with the rationale that this would most likely be our last baby.

Our family size was a perfect match for many of the accommodations we encountered in our society.

From dining room sets to the midsize sedan automobiles, the "seating for four" concept is well established.

For us to exceed this norm by adding just one more child to our family unit would needlessly upset the balance of my organized life. Why would I do that when it felt so good to have my reproductive obligation checked off of my to-do list? I embraced my perceived right to be free to move on and raise our two rambunctious boys as

---

7. Humphrey Taylor, "New Harris Poll Finds Different Religious Groups Have Very Different Attitudes to Some Health Policies and Programs," Harris Interactive, www.harrisinteractive .com, October 20, 2005.

best I could. I was quite happy to say that on the birthing aspect of my motherhood vocation, I was "done."

Or was I?

A Providential Fishing Trip | *Greg*

I don't get to go fishing very often, but when I do, apparently it makes me open to new ideas.

Back in 2001 (the same year the U.S. census confirmed we had more than enough children), I went fishing with my brother Paul in South Carolina and had a fantastic time. We caught hardly anything, but we did spend twelve hours in a boat, drinking beer. So I'd say the trip was a success.

I planned on driving home early the next morning so I could make it back in time for Sunday Mass, but my brother convinced me we should get on the water one more time before I left. That morning we did indeed catch some mammoth large-mouth bass, which made the trip even more exciting.

Then I got on the road, made it home, got cleaned up, and rushed off with Jennifer and our boys to the one 5 PM Mass offered on Sundays in our area. I mention this because we hardly ever went to that particular Mass. It changed our lives forever.

In the homily, Deacon Jack Jansen (God rest his soul) told us about being the father of nine children. He talked not only about the Church's teachings in regard to being open to life but also the reasons behind what the Church teaches.

Jennifer and I squirmed in our seats a little. We already felt completely overwhelmed with the two children we had. Having a third (or more) was just crazy talk.

23

As a cradle Catholic, I'd been taught that contraception was bad, but no one had ever bothered to explain *why* it was sinful. Jennifer and I had been treating it as an option in our marriage. I simply chose, for many years, to ignore the little prompting in my brain that knew it was wrong.

But Deacon Jack's words resonated with me. He spoke not just about having a bunch of kids but of trusting God. It didn't matter if God blessed us with one kid, twenty kids, or no kids at all. What Deacon Jack stressed was the importance of knowing that God will take care of all of our needs no matter what, that God gives us children as a blessing—a gift—and that children help us grow closer to God.

Were my children truly gifts, or were they curses?

With every fiber of my being I knew they were gifts, of course. And what fool in his right mind would refuse a gift from God? Does God know what's best for us or not?

That crazy talk was making sense.

The *Catechism* says that

> the innate language that expresses the total reciprocal self-giving of husband and wife is overlaid, through contraception, by an objectively contradictory language, namely, that of not giving oneself totally to the other. This leads not only to a positive refusal to be open to life but also to a falsification of the inner truth of conjugal love, which is called upon to give itself in personal totality. (*CCC*, 2370)

Initially, when I read that statement, I just saw the scary words: *contraception, contradictory, not giving oneself totally, refusal, falsification.*

But when I read through it again, I saw the positive angle for the first time: "total reciprocal self-giving of husband and wife," "giving oneself totally to the other," "open to life," "inner truth of conjugal love," "give itself in personal totality."

Deacon Jack clinched the deal by giving us a website to check out. If you tell me about a website, I pretty much can't help myself. I'll at least give it a look (unless, of course, it's a porn site or something stupid like that). The website he suggested addressed the idea of chastity as something not just for unmarried people but for married couples too.

Chastity in marriage? Are you kidding? That sounded really crazy. I got married so I wouldn't *have* to be chaste!

Later I sat in our living room looking at the website Deacon Jack had recommended. Then the positive side of being open to life—of rejecting contraception and following the centuries-old teaching of the Church—started to sink in.

Contraception Misconception | *Jennifer*

The website was www.thinkchastity.com, and my husband had suddenly seen the light. Next thing you know, I was in a serious discussion with Greg about our Catholic faith's teaching on birth control.

Needless to say, it was not a pretty meeting.

After all, I wanted full control of my right to reproduce.

My body. My choice. My right. End of story.

By this time Greg and I had tried several forms of contraception. I had gone from using the standard birth-control pill to experimenting with the Depo-Provera injection. Interestingly enough, I always hated being on those synthetic drugs. I never felt quite like myself. I eventually was fed up with the side effects—crankiness and bloating and generally feeling terrible—and opted to take myself off of them. I craved a return to my body's natural way of regulating its hormones.

My desire was for better physical health; Greg and I never considered the possibility that it was sinful behavior.

Greg had picked up the contraception mantle. At this point we felt a tug on our conscience and decided to double-check with a priest friend of ours that we were not in fact doing anything sinful. Being newly brought into full communion with the Church, I honestly did not know what the Church taught about it. Greg knew so many "good" Catholics who were using contraception that he was confused on the issue. Later he'd admit that he willfully opted to remain unclear as to why it was wrong.

When we met with the priest we knew, he told us that on the matter of contraception we could "let our conscience be our guide." That was it. No mention of natural family planning. No mention of the *Catechism's* blatant statement that contraception is "intrinsically evil" (*CCC*, 2370). Just decide for yourselves.

My reaction to this priest's spiritual advice was relief. But when I think back to what he said that day, I am filled with deep sadness. It doesn't take a rocket scientist to figure out what decision we were going to make based on his giving us permission to carry on our contraceptive course. Now I pray for that priest and others like him who have failed to properly instruct misguided people like us. Thank goodness, our Lord did not allow us to remain on that path of death for very long.

Why did we originally want contraception in our marriage?

Because we bought into the idea that marital relations with no consequences of pregnancy were a right and privilege we could enjoy as a married couple. Sex was as normal as breathing. It was meant for fun, and for children only when *we* wanted children.

I subscribed to the world's norms on what an appropriate family size would be. Again, that would be 1.91 kids, and we'd already exceeded that goal. I couldn't have had my priorities more distorted.

Now here was Greg telling me I needed to be open to life and to this papal encyclical called *Humanae Vitae*. Weren't documents like *Humanae Vitae* akin to assigned reading for advanced Catholics only? Couldn't I be a good *à la carte* Catholic? Isn't it better to be choosy when visiting the cafeteria rather than eating everything at the buffet?

The quick answer to those questions was obviously yes—if I wanted to settle for a life of spiritual imperfection.

Who Still Has a Cassette Player? | *Greg*

Deacon Jack's was the most succinctly preached homily I'd ever heard on the subject of being open to life. When I told him after Mass how his words had moved me, he went out to his car and got a cassette tape of a talk by Dr. Janet Smith called "Contraception: Why Not?" I would listen to it more than once during my commute to work that week. I was shocked at the countless examples Dr. Smith provided of couples whose marriages were strengthened not because they had multiple children but because they were open to God working in every aspect of their lives. Conversely, she talked about the statistics that conclusively prove the damage that contraception brings to marriages.[8]

Suddenly there were several new questions that I had no choice but to answer.

Did I want to love Jennifer more, totally and completely? Or did I want to create barriers—whether chemical or physical—between us? Were we really inviting God 100 percent into our marriage, or were we blocking him out by attempting to render sterile what he created?

---

8. Dr. Janet Smith's talk "Contraception: Why Not?" is available on CD. This and other helpful materials are available at her website, www.janetsmith.org.

I liked to think that I was totally open with Jennifer, that we were always completely honest with each other, that we gave ourselves completely to each other.

But that was a lie.

The truth was, in using contraception, we were trying to control each other. In essence contraception allowed us to objectify each other, to use the sexual act for pleasure alone.

The two primary purposes of the conjugal act are unitive and procreative. How could it be unitive if we weren't giving ourselves 100 percent in that unity?

And obviously it couldn't be procreative if we were blocking out any chances of procreation.

Did I love my wife completely or not?

If I was not willing to accept 100 percent of my wife—and that included accepting her God-given fertility—then I absolutely could not continue to hold true to the claim that I loved her completely.

Therefore the act, even in marriage, was void of purity. As long as we were taking steps away from fully embracing each other, we were essentially kicking God out into the hallway.

I now understood that, through our use of contraception, I was in a state of grave sin. And I was bringing my wife down with me.

Humanae Vitae in One Hundred Words or Less
(or More) | *Jennifer*

Now what would we do?

Greg gave me a summary of *Humanae Vitae*, and my soul could not deny the wisdom I was hearing. I had to respond. I had to honor the wisdom of the Church's teaching against contraception, not out of a sense of obligation but because of the love and freedom the Church wanted me to enjoy.

After much prayer, I challenged myself with difficult questions. I knew deep down that God was calling me, as he has all of us, to be "holy, for I the LORD your God am holy" (Leviticus 19:2), and again, to be "perfect, as your heavenly Father is perfect" (Matthew 5:48). God was challenging me to strive for perfection not just on one day but for every day that I'm alive. I had to understand that his level of holiness and perfection was not unattainable but, in actuality, rooted in his love. Learning to love the way he loves us is the key to holiness.

Admitting that I had issues with the Catholic Church's teaching on contraception highlighted an area of spiritual weakness on my part, but with God's gentle loving guidance, he has helped me overcome that weakness. You may have a different imperfection altogether. Is it jealousy? Greed? Inability to control your anger? Sexual impurity? Those aren't the fruits of the Holy Spirit.

The *fruits* of the Spirit are perfections that the Holy Spirit forms in us as the firstfruits of eternal glory. These are what allow us to have self-control, not only in areas of chastity but in other areas of our lives where we face weaknesses. The Church lists twelve of them: charity, joy, peace, patience, kindness, goodness, generosity, gentleness, faithfulness, modesty, self-control, chastity (*CCC*, 1832; see Galatians 5:22–23).

The astounding variety of moral imperfections, including their varying degrees of severity, continually reminds me of how our selfish natures constantly try to assume control of our hearts and minds. We must learn how to handle the confrontation with the truth about ourselves and then invite God in for some spiritual surgery.

chapter four

NFP FOR YOU AND ME

Charting a Plan | *Jennifer*

When I came into full communion with the Catholic Church back in 1999, I made a commitment to live according to the teachings of Christ and his holy Catholic Church, not according to the wisdom of the world. From childhood I knew that God's ways were not like the ways of man (see Isaiah 55:8).

When the dignity of life is in question, the wisdom of the Church is the only place to get the hard and sometimes uncomfortable truth.

If Greg and I hadn't heard Deacon Jack's homily those many years ago, who knows how long we would have continued on our misguided path?

How was I to undo my former mind-set? I knew I needed to learn more about the Church's teaching on family planning. But I'll be honest with you, it was a frustratingly slow process of enlightenment, especially since the opportunities for physical marital bonding were ever present.

While I do not condone gratuitous violence in movies, I did enjoy one aspect of the movie *The Matrix*. It was the part of the film where Keanu Reeves's character plugged into the back of his head a cable that allowed him to receive in a matter of minutes full knowledge of complex concepts and requisite skills. That scene is embedded in my mind as a fantasy situation for learning anything. I wish I could simply wirelessly download all of Christ's teachings, along with the ability to live out those teachings, in a few minutes.

But no, I have to learn it all the good old-fashioned way—by reading and questioning and struggling to get specific answers to questions that matter to me or *should* matter to me.

Back in 2002 we started our new journey of more fully living out the teachings of the Church by signing up for a class on natural family planning (NFP) that met on Saturdays. We purchased our required NFP book, *The Art of Natural Family Planning*, which read a bit like a biology textbook.[9] We went to our first class filled with hopes for a brighter future in this part of our intimate lives. We hoped to more fully invite God into our marriage.

What we got instead was a shock to our system.

After an overview of the current methods of approved NFP, we were taught the symptothermal method, which was the particular method taught in that class. There we were hit with a bombshell: Starting right then, we had to abstain from relations for thirty days so that I could observe and chart my first cycle.

"What do you mean, abstain?" we asked the instructor, with a distinct "how dare you" tone in our question.

Of course, we knew what *abstain* meant, but we hoped to somehow be wrong in our understanding of the word. We weren't. We went home dubious but determined to try.

So began a very difficult thirty days. We were young and spiritually immature, and we had already experienced years of sex whenever we wanted with the use of contraception.

No less than forty-eight hours into the thirty-day period, we were

---

9. John and Sheila Kippley, *The Art of Natural Family Planning*, 4th ed. (Cincinnati: Couple to Couple League, 1996).

questioning the validity of this symptothermal method.

"Did we hear the teachers correctly?" Greg would ask. "Maybe they said *three* days."

Despite the tension and misery— more physically felt by Greg and emotionally felt by me—we did survive. And we grew closer together, just as we'd been promised. This challenging experience gave us time to more greatly appreciate the precious gift of our sexuality and to more fully appreciate each other.

Certainly, learning to live with NFP in those early days brought some struggles in our marriage, mostly because of our lack of understanding even after the classes were completed.

We didn't have access to adequate resources to answer our "private" questions. The questions we repeatedly found ourselves asking began like this: "If we do ——— during fertile times, are we still in compliance with abstinence?" Or like teenagers we'd ask, "Exactly how far *can* we go without compromising our decision to abstain?"

This was well before Bl. Pope John Paul II's theology of the body registered on my radar. It seemed that no matter how hard I searched, I was never able to find a Frequently Asked Questions brochure that would answer specific intimate questions of this nature.

Let's just say that we made many mistakes in our early attempts at being chaste within our marriage. Even now, years later, we continue to learn what it truly means to love as God does. Our marriage, like our faith, is a continuous journey. Life always places us in unpredictable situations that challenge our abilities to love, especially within our marriage.

Over the course of the next several years, our NFP method did change as a result of further study.

In 2010 we were properly introduced to the Marquette method of NFP and have been enjoying it ever since.[10] Now we continue to regularly have discussions and pray about when to welcome new life in a way that is rooted in honesty and dignity. Our desire is to fully include God in all aspects of our marriage.

We are complying with my body's natural cycles of fertility and infertility while remaining open to new life, and our marriage has never been better.

Theology of the Body in a Nutshell | Greg

Over the years we've found that the more we learn about our bodies as God made them, and the more we respect them as such, the greater our love for each other grows.

The term "theology of the body" gets thrown around a lot, almost as an interchangeable term for "natural family planning." But the two are different though compatible subjects. Whereas NFP is a method of moderating births that is completely in compliance with Church teaching, theology of the body is an integrated vision of the human person—body, soul, and spirit.

Bl. John Paul II developed these teachings in a series of one hundred twenty-nine Wednesday audiences between 1979 and 1984. Drawing from Scripture and tradition, he provided an understanding of what it means to be created in God's image. Understanding that helps us to better understand the differences between the sexes and the uniqueness of each sex.

It is that idea of the uniqueness of each sex that I love the most. That God specifically made me to be one way, and for one purpose, and that he made my wife to be another way, and for another

---

10. Information about the Marquette method of NFP is available at http://nfp.marquette.edu.

purpose—neither one greater than the other—I find to be one of the most beautiful things I've ever come to understand.

God made my wife fully woman and made me fully man, and he made us both fully complementary, for love and procreation. We are equal but not the same, and that is his grand design.

Why on earth would I want to modify either myself or my wife to serve any other purpose? That's what contraception in all of its forms does. It modifies us away from the way God intended us to be. Contraception is like going out and buying a top-of-the-line Ferrari, removing the round tires, and putting square blocks on instead. It just doesn't make sense.

Free to Love | *Jennifer*

Now that I understand our responsibility to love one another completely, right down to our God-given fertility, I see contraception as a disease that is infecting our culture. Some methods alter female hormonal chemistry, others are types of reproductive mutilation, and others present physical barriers to conception. But all have the same goal: to prevent life-giving love and to redefine conception as an unwelcome and negative consequence.

How unjust it is to label an innocent baby as a negative consequence.

Behold, sons are a heritage from the LORD,
   the fruit of the womb a reward.
Like arrows in the hand of a warrior
   are the sons of one's youth.
Happy is the man who has
   his quiver full of them!
He shall not be put to shame
   when he speaks with his enemies in the gate. (Psalm 127:3–5)

Is the Church saying that all married couples must procreate constantly? Must all Catholic families have ten children in order to be in good standing? No. The Church is only saying that we must remain open to new life whenever we choose to engage in sexual relations with our spouses.

The *Catechism of the Catholic Church* teaches that "the regulation of births represents one of the aspects of responsible fatherhood and motherhood. Legitimate intentions on the part of the spouses do not justify recourse to morally unacceptable means (for example, direct sterilization or contraception)" (*CCC,* 2399).

This is very different from saying, "Thou shalt have a minimum of ten children."

Remember, God has arranged the woman's cycle to include a discernible window of infertility. If a married couple have a serious reason to avoid pregnancy, they simply abstain from sexual relations during the time of fertility, which could range from four to nine days. During that brief period of abstinence, the couple have a wonderful opportunity to explore nonsexual love for one another.

I Hate Waiting | *Greg*
Let me chime in here briefly for all men whose wives have brought this book to them and commanded, "Read this part."

This is your affirmation:

Abstinence is tough.

Now, here's something to consider:

Abstinence is awesome too, because when you've been through the desert, that drink of water at the oasis is unlike any other.

If you're using contraception in your marriage, it's easy to start taking your spouse for granted. We can assume that sex is always available as a way to relieve ourselves from the tensions caused by those Hooters billboards and other perversions society throws at us. And with contraception, that's all it is. Sex.

Remember on your honeymoon—after the wedding ceremony, after the reception, after the guests—when it was just you and your spouse? The two of you looked at each other, and then you kissed. Remember that electricity? Remember the jolt of anticipation as you realized your wait was now over and you were finally husband and wife and could be together completely?

If you're using contraception, when was the last time you felt that?

But if you abstain, you get that feeling every month. You can feel the electricity, the excitement, the purity, and the righteousness that you experienced the first time you and your spouse made love.

When you say no to contraception, you're always open to God blessing you with a miracle. But if you find yourself in a troublesome situation in life, such as job loss or other issues that make it imprudent for now to welcome a new member to your family, you can work in cooperation with the way God made your spouse's body.

It's no fun to wait, but for Jennifer and me our periods of abstinence are usually the times when we talk more, rekindle our love, and remind one another how to show genuine affection and be the husband and wife God meant for us to be. By respecting the fertility God gave us, our marriage is one of constant renewal.

It's tough to wait, but the reward is awesome.

Are You Serious? | *Jennifer*

One popular question Catholics ask is, "What constitutes a serious reason to avoid a pregnancy?" Because words like *serious* can be relative in nature, the reasons to abstain can vary greatly from one couple to the next.

Seeking spiritual guidance from a priest who knows and supports the teachings of the Church, in addition to using resources like the *Catechism of the Catholic Church*, will help couples understand whether their personal reasons to avoid pregnancy are actually serious and not born out of selfishness. The biggest question a couple needs to answer is "Why would we *not* welcome new life this month?" Then put the answer to that question to a type of selfishness test.

If your reason is no deeper than just "not feeling like dealing with a baby," then you may be avoiding pregnancy for the wrong reasons.

The Church cannot provide absolute reasons for avoiding pregnancy, because no one set of reasons would apply to all the cases that different couples may present. The Church can only guide with some examples, such as the physical and psychological health of the mother and poor financial situations. If legitimate reasons such as those exist, then the couple can appropriately make use of NFP.

When I was trying to wrap my brain around this teaching of being open to life and of avoiding use of contraceptives, I thought that the Church was trying to force me into having more kids than I believed I could handle. That honestly made me angry. It took me a few years to understand that the Church wanted me to simply relax, be open to trusting God with my fertility, and cooperate with my own body's natural cycles of fertility and infertility. To abstain from relations with the proper interior disposition, during times when we prayerfully discern that raising a new baby would not be prudent, will result in the perfect family size.

It is also important to point out that there are times when a pregnancy will result even though the couple chose to avoid it. There can be a variety of reasons for this. For example, the woman might err in her fertile observations; this is more likely to occur when a couple have not been properly educated in NFP. Or perhaps extensive travel makes it difficult for her to observe and chart her fertile signs accurately. No matter the case, if a pregnancy should occur, our Catholic teaching guides us to the proper response: to trust in God's providence and welcome that new life as a gift.

This is at the very heart of being open to life.

Greg and I have had four unplanned pregnancies in our marriage to date. In other words, we were given four opportunities to respond to this life-changing news. To each of those surprise pregnancies, our response was embarrassingly the same—shock followed by a brief period of frustration over not being ready to welcome another child. But in each situation, we at least went to our Father in prayer with our worries. After that, we were able to turn our frustration into joyful anticipation for the new lives to come. But just because we were open to life doesn't mean we were guaranteed to get it.

Three of the four pregnancies resulted in miscarriages. While it wasn't easy to see God's blessings immediately after the miscarriages happened, we see them now when we look back on those difficult moments in our marriage. We will never know exactly why God chose to reclaim those newly created souls back to him, but one fact remains clear: He granted me the privilege of welcoming and providing a home for them inside my own womb. He gave me the chance to bond with those babies if only for two months at a time. He gave me the chance to once again marvel at his creative power. Instead of mothering those three children for countless years, I was given eight precious weeks. Eight weeks that I will cherish for the rest of my life.

Much to our surprise, the third unplanned pregnancy resulted in a beautiful and healthy baby girl, our fifth child and first daughter, Lily.

It's truly difficult to express the pure and innocent joy that has come from her presence in our family. God knew what he was doing by surprising us with this beautiful gift. And all of the reasons we had for not getting pregnant at that time were later proven to be completely unfounded.

Who am I to ever say, "The number of children in my family shall not exceed two (or four, or six)"?

God knows what the perfect number is for my family, as he does for your family. He only asks us to be obedient to him and to trust him with this part of our lives.

NFP is not about following a set of rules but about being in love with God and wanting to cooperate with him in planning our family.

By doing so, we open ourselves up to graces and blessings that give us joy in this fallen world and help us get through any challenges that raising children may bring. Simply put, if we obey and trust him in everything, even the area of our fertility, he *will* provide.

chapter five

WE'RE MORE IMPORTANT THAN YOU ARE

Field Trip Breakdown | *Jennifer*

Mmmmm. There's nothing quite like the flavor of one-year-old freezer-burned wedding cake. Isn't that what most married couples eat at their one-year anniversary mark?

When I reflect back on the way Greg and I spent our first anniversary, I am amazed at what we were able to accomplish. A couple's massage, leisurely shopping, gourmet dining—we reveled in celebrating ourselves. After all, isn't successfully completing one year of marriage something to celebrate?

Sadly, God was not at the center of that first year of marriage, as he could have been. I suppose we were both so distracted with "playing grown-up for real" that we did not immediately see the importance of making God an active part of our lives. At best, God was the elephant in the room. We both knew he was there, we both knew we should be paying more attention to him and allowing him to be a bigger part of our lives and our marriage, but we continued to dance around him and focus on nothing but ourselves.

Fast-forward fifteen years, and our wedding anniversary looked like this:

"Boys! It's time to load up in the van! Make sure you go to the bathroom first!!"

"Honey, where's the diaper bag?"

"Greg, do you have the tickets?"

"I thought *you* had the tickets!"

"OK, kids! Stop number one, the Atlanta zoo!"

Yes, the zoo. Nowhere near as glamorous as the gourmet restaurant or the couple's massage fourteen years before, but definitely a reflection of our current state in life.

When we were deliberating over how to spend this wedding anniversary, we didn't feel right about leaving the kids with babysitters while we pampered ourselves, even for an accomplishment like fifteen years of marriage. So we decided to purchase a city pass that would allow our entire family of seven admission to six major attractions in the Atlanta area. In other words, our fifteenth anniversary was turned into a field-trip marathon with five young children in tow.

After two consecutive ten-hour days of walking, exploring and dining out with all the kids, both Greg and I felt oddly defeated and worn out. Zoo Atlanta, the CNN studio tour, the Georgia Aquarium, and the World of Coca-Cola Museum were not meant to be visited with four young boys and a toddler, all inside of forty-eight hours. What were we thinking? Naturally, crabbiness set in as the physical exhaustion of our days took its toll on all of us, including the kids.

From my front passenger seat in our Cheerios-filled minivan on the way home after the second day of family outings, I took one look behind me and saw five sweaty and red-cheeked kids, exhausted from the trek and ready for a junk-food solution to dinner. To my left was my equally worn-out husband holding on to the steering wheel with whatever energy he could muster. His entire body conveyed one single message: Just…get…*home.*

And then one of us (I don't remember who) said, "I wish both you and I could have had some alone time together for our fifteenth wedding anniversary." It was as if we were reading each other's minds. We both clearly realized we'd made an error in planning the full celebration of our life of sacramental marriage. While we agreed that sharing this event with the kids was both fun and wise, it was not good to brush off our desire for that romantic getaway to refresh and renew our spirits. While family is of the utmost importance, if we didn't also spend time together, we couldn't possibly be there for the family.

We were early in our return journey home from the big city, and I had approximately thirty-five minutes on this Friday afternoon in mid-September to arrange a romantic getaway for two. Just thirty-five minutes to find a child-care solution and to book reservations at a hotel somewhere in the state of Georgia. I rose to the challenge. Greg's countenance lifted as he allowed his mind to ponder the possibilities of making this last-minute decision a reality.

But could I pull it off?

I silently prayed that God would open the doors for us. If not, then we would simply accept our situation and count our blessings. Armed with my iPhone, I set to work nailing down the most difficult detail of our romantic itinerary: a babysitter who would be able to come into our home on short notice and play live-in nanny for a couple of days. Within twenty-five minutes or so came the text message from Miss Christy, one of our favorite family helpers, with a resounding *yes*.

In the next couple of hours, Greg and I drew on a newfound energy as we joyfully packed our bags in preparation for our romantic bed-and-breakfast getaway for two in Atlanta. Thanks be to God, we were going to celebrate our marriage and refresh our hearts, minds, and souls.

Focusing on the Family | *Greg*

The difference between how we celebrated our first anniversary and how we celebrated our fifteenth is significant for two major reasons.

First and foremost, over those first fifteen years of marriage, through Jennifer's full communion with the Catholic Church as an adult and my own reawakened faith, we'd come to the conclusion that God had to be at the center of our marriage. We realized we were doomed unless God played an active part in every single aspect of our family life. That realization would later have repercussions in many positive ways.

Second, after having five children, we'd also grown to understand how, while focusing on the kids is important, if our marriage is weak, our family is weak, and in turn our kids will be weak. Selfish as it may sound, our marriage must come before the children, because a strong marriage will ultimately strengthen our children as well.

On our fifteenth anniversary, while our intent was good (spending quality time with the kids), the reality is that our marriage was in desperate need of some tending to as well. Going overboard in doing things with the kids knocked us off balance, which manifested in short, sharp sentences to each other and a general "shutting down" of our ability to be open and affectionate.

A few years ago there was a popular television reality show called *Jon and Kate Plus Eight*, which focused on a couple and their eight children—a set of twins and a younger set of sextuplets.

We enjoyed watching occasional episodes of this program during the early run, when the focus was on the joys and trials of raising active young children. But slowly it developed into a weekly showcase of various field trips and extravagant vacations that we knew our family would never be able to afford. Despite my enjoyment of the early days of the program, I cringed uncomfortably every time the couple repeated their mantra: "This is all about the kids. The kids always come first. We do all this for the kids."

It was evident, and I have no doubt, that Jon and Kate Gosselin loved their kids as much as they said. But the reality is that they were putting the wrong people first. Over the course of several seasons, the tabloids in the grocery-store checkout lines reported month after nauseating month of Jon and Kate's marriage breakdown. Eventually the couple publicly announced their separation and later their divorce.

In our family we try to live by the motto that after our relationship with God comes our marriage. We love our children completely, but the way we show them how much we love them is by doing everything we can to maintain the strength and stability of our marriage.

If our marriage is weak, our family is weak. If our marriage becomes fractured, our family becomes fractured. Strong families and strong children come from strong marriages.

The best way to put children first is to actually put them second, behind a strong sacramental marriage.

Things We Do to Keep Our Marriage Healthy | *Jennifer*
The kids are finally in bed. The sounds of laughter, yelling, door slams, and crying are now fading memories. My dear husband is sitting comatose on the couch, staring at the television, pondering the difficult decision of what television program to watch for our evening entertainment. I have just enough energy to walk over and join him.

"Popcorn?" Greg mumbles.

"Hmmm," I reply. "OK, I guess."

We mindlessly munch on our evening snack, and when the bowl is empty the TV goes off and we head for bed. The hour is usually something like 10:30 PM. After five minutes of light reading, the lights go out, and soon after so does our consciousness.

It would be very easy to allow each day's commitments to rule the roost. There are times when the routine of it all can actually provide a level of comfort. What I would like to suggest is that you don't allow this comfort of the home life—the routines and everyday obligations—to lead to neglect of regular one-on-one time with your spouse.

Every couple is different with respect to which activities they enjoy. Some couples are the hiking type, others the bowling type, others the road tripping type, and so on. It's important to take time to explore what common interests you have and then participate in those activities, remembering to reexplore those interests every few years to see if they've changed with time and circumstances.

After our first two children joined our family and the busyness of life and parenting set in, I was disappointed that when we had the opportunity for time as a couple, Greg and I couldn't think of any activity besides the typical movie date. I felt dissatisfied with the amount of marital bonding we shared outside of the marital embrace.

Sure, we went out to eat on special occasions when we were fortunate enough to find an available babysitter, but was that enough to keep the marriage healthy? Sharing a latte at the local coffeehouse was a lovely retreat from the day-to-day grind, but was that enough to stoke the fires of our marital love? Was it wrong of me to want more for us?

God put this desire deep within us, this yearning, because, if followed through properly, it can yield much fruit in our marriage. In fact, the *Catechism of the Catholic Church* continuously refers to the various fruits that are produced within marriage.

CCC, 1615: This grace of Christian marriage is a fruit of Christ's cross, the source of all Christian life.

CCC, 1642: *Christ is the source of this grace.* "Just as of old God encountered his people with a covenant of love and fidelity, so our Savior, the spouse of the Church, now encounters Christian spouses through the sacrament of Matrimony" [*Gaudium et Spes,* 48.2]. Christ dwells with them, gives them the strength to take up their crosses and so follow him, to rise again after they have fallen, to forgive one another, to bear one another's burdens, to "be subject to one another out of reverence for Christ" [Ephesians 5:21; cf. Galatians 6:2], and to love one another with supernatural, tender, and fruitful love.

CCC, 1662: Marriage is based on the consent of the contracting parties, that is, on their will to give themselves, each to the other, mutually and definitively, in order to live a covenant of faithful and fruitful love.

And there are many examples beyond those.

Any activity that affirms and nurtures the sacramentality of marriage is an activity worth pursuing. This is great news, because the possibilities are many when looked at in this light. Whether you're cooking a challenging recipe together at home, embarking on a romantic cruise, nursing a sick child, or struggling through unemployment or other loss, you can affirm your marriage if you have the right mind-set.

I believe understanding and learning that mind-set is critical. Rather than telling you it's all about loving the other person, I'd like to offer it another way.

Love is involved, of course, but more important here is how you love.

The marriage-affirming mind-set is about completely loving the personhood of your spouse for the simple reason that that's how God loves that person. It's a decision on your part to love your spouse no matter what and to love in an active way.

Not in Love Anymore? | *Greg*
Recently a caller on our radio program told us about a married couple who were ready to call it quits. As a last resort they went to a priest.

"Father," the husband said, "I just don't love my wife anymore."

"Then love her," the priest said.

"You obviously didn't hear me," the man replied. "I don't love her anymore."

"Then love her," the priest repeated.

"But I don't love her anymore."

One last time the priest told him, "If you don't love her, then *love* her."

Love is not just a noun that describes a feeling of elation and tingling excitement.

Love is a verb. Love is an action. Love is a decision we have to actively make each and every second within the sacrament of marriage.

If you struggle with loving your spouse, pick up your cross and turn your love into an action. Love your spouse through continuous acts of love and service.

Still Giddy in Love | *Jennifer*
The most amazing thing happens in a marriage when a couple learns to pay attention to how they love each other. Suddenly you become

giddy over how you can please your spouse throughout multiple moments in your day.

Love begets more love.

It grows exponentially with each act of love.

It's what makes marriage so awesome.

God planned it that way. Love is akin to a drop of heaven we get to taste while living in this broken world.

I think every married couple should have a date night of sorts every week, if possible. Those date nights could be celebrated either at home or outside the home, just as long as they include only the two of you. It's also healthy to take at least a twenty-four-hour period of time alone together once every few months. And finally, married couples benefit greatly from traveling together, either on a pilgrimage or a vacation-style excursion, once every year or two.

Financial restraints and other commitments can make these kinds of getaways challenging, but we've experienced firsthand (as have our children) their benefits. The refreshment one receives from the change of scenery simply cannot be underestimated, both for the individual soul and for the marriage. And while financial concerns often prohibit travel, creativity and prayer can find worthy substitutes. We've discovered that this is one of those prayers that God often answers, because these times of intimacy are so affirming for our marriage.

I used to feel guilty about leaving the kids behind for a quick getaway. (Truth be told, I still feel that way sometimes.) I thought that I was somehow a bad parent even if I left them in the capable hands of loving family members. I felt that I had to be the martyr-mommy. But the only result of that mind-set was a perpetually exhausted woman who was too tired to pay much attention to her husband when he came home and too cranky to be an effective mother.

That doesn't sound too marriage-affirming to me.

If you're married, when was the last time you had a getaway with your spouse?

Following Good Examples | *Greg*

Between Jennifer's parents and my parents, we have been blessed with beautiful examples of nearly one hundred years of marriage. This number is startling to me but also incredibly affirming in many ways.

My life was very simple growing up. We weren't poor, but neither were we rich. My parents, and my mother especially, were always very frugal. They didn't shower me with tons of gifts, nor did they allow me to join every club I wanted to join.

Instead they encouraged (not forced) me to hold my first job, delivering newspapers, when I was ten years old, simultaneously teaching me the value of a dollar while fostering responsibility in me, which was far more beneficial.

Now, as a parent of multiple children, I see the wisdom of my parents' not allowing my siblings and me to join too many clubs and organizations. Instead we participated in many home activities, and my parents were not strained beyond reason in a quest to develop well-rounded kids through extracurricular activities. We became well-rounded in other ways.

I also had the example of my parents spending time together. When I was in kindergarten, my parents went to Italy—without any of their six kids. More than thirty years later my mom still says she feels guilty about that, but I've also had a lifetime of listening to my parents tell stories of that trip.

They took many other trips together, sometimes quick weekend jaunts as a part of my dad's work, and other times, when finances allowed, slightly more extravagant getaways.

There were also family road trips, certainly. But my parents were big believers in having time away from their children.

At home we had set bedtimes, and my parents went out for date nights regularly. It's not that they didn't love us. It's that they *did* love us, so they took the extra effort to focus on their marriage. The Catholic Church teaches that "the well-being of the individual person and of both human and Christian society is closely bound up with the healthy state of conjugal and family life" (*CCC*, 1603, citing *Gaudium et Spes* 47.1).

But vacations and date nights alone don't make a solid marriage. I also have countless memories of my parents' joint and individual efforts to focus on God. Many mornings I would walk into the living room to find both of them quietly drinking coffee and reading from their well-used Bibles.

I remember weekends with just one parent at home as the other worked at or participated in a spiritual retreat. Many a time they would come home, from a Cursillo or other retreat, exuberant and renewed in their fervor for God and each other.

Years later, following my parents' example, both Jennifer and I attended Cursillo weekends. We continue to seek out spiritual retreats, knowing of the benefit to ourselves, our marriage, and our children.

Another example my parents gave me was in the area of hospitality. They would often invite people into our home for dinner. Charity was their common theme.

My siblings and their families are now scattered around the country, but in December of 2006 we all came together to celebrate my parents' fiftieth wedding anniversary. It was the first time in nearly two decades that the six of us kids, as well as our spouses and children, were all together. We watched our parents stand at the altar and renew their sacramental vows to each other.

If my parents had placed all the focus on us kids, I don't believe they would have made it. They focused on their marriage. And not only did they strengthen their own bond, but they taught me innumerable lessons about love that to this day I strive to live in my own marriage.

Resources for Strong Marriages | *Jennifer*
There are so many ways, both simple and complex, in which we can strengthen our marriages. Here are some of my favorites.

Staying as close to God as I can through prayer
Going to eucharistic adoration
Going to confession
Never missing Sunday Mass except for a grave reason
Taking the time to understand my Catholic faith
Being open to life
Having heart-to-heart conversations with my husband
Sharing intimacy with him
Being the best mother I can be to our children
Letting Greg know that he has my support in everything, but having the courage to lovingly correct him if and when he needs it
Cooking meals for him, so he doesn't have to worry about preparing them himself
Giving him opportunities to get away from the house by himself with no strings attached
Being a compassionate listener when he talks to me about anything

Allowing him to express his anger and frustration over situations in life without taking his anger personally

Sharing any meal together

Exchanging a knowing glance with each other over a chaotic dinner with our children

Getting away from the responsibilities of work, home, and children for a couple of days with no one but Greg

Attempting to sing cover songs in harmony over piano or guitar

Laughing with Greg before we fall asleep

No matter how old your kids are, whether they are small and living with you or they are grown and gone, loving the complete personhood of your spouse is an absolute must to keeping your marriage thriving. It orients all of your actions toward loving charity.

There are wonderful resources that can help you build and even repair your marriage. For Your Marriage is an invaluable resource for couples who are either dating, engaged, or married. This site, ForYour Marriage.org, sponsored and operated by the United States Conference of Catholic Bishops, is beautifully organized and presented. There is something for everyone here, and it's worth a visit to learn more about having the best marriage possible. The site even includes a marriage-assessment tool that, given the honest answers you provide, rates the current strength of your marriage.

Marriage Encounter is a weekend program designed to improve the communication and love between married couples. For more information, visit www.wwme.org.

Engaged Encounter is a weekend retreat to plan for a sacramental marriage. It is designed to give couples the opportunity to dialogue honestly and intensively about their strengths and weaknesses, their desires and ambitions, their role in the Church and society, and their attitudes about money, sex, children, and family.

There are marriages that suffer bitterly as a consequence of sinful or simply selfish actions. If this describes your marriage, you need to know that there is hope. *Retrouvaille*, a French word for "rediscovery," is a reputable and trusted Christian organization that is dedicated to offering a saving lifeline to marriages that may be headed for divorce. The program is offered for both Catholic and non-Catholic Christians.

Another highly sought after marriage saving resource is an organization called The Alexander House founded by Greg and Julie Alexander. This international organization is dedicated to saving couples who believe they are destined for divorce.

chapter six
MY KIDS MADE A MOM OUT OF ME

Just What Do They Think They're Doing? | *Jennifer*

There are many angles I could take to describe the joys and trials of motherhood. There are as many questions I could ask myself about whether I am living up to my potential as a mom. But what I would rather mention here are a few noteworthy examples of how my kids have helped me to grow in holiness. Please note, I am far from perfect. But each day I accept God's help and wind up learning more about myself through the adventures of raising children.

It took me several years of being a mother to realize what my kids were really doing to me. While there were plenty of days when they drove me a little crazy, more often than not they drove me to my knees in prayer. And that's not a bad way for me to spend my time.

When I am willing to see it, my kids give me important clues as to how God sees me. Just as Sam, Walt, Ben, Tom, and Lily are related to me as my biological children, I relate to God as his spiritual child. When one of my kids throws a tantrum in front of me because I denied him or her something that wouldn't be good in the long run, I get a glimpse of how I might look in God's eyes whenever he denies me something for my own good. Just when I think my parenting role gives me sole authority to teach my kids, I am regularly taught by them in the most profound of ways.

Even as I sit to write this chapter, I've got kids coming into my workspace to ask about snacks for their unending appetites or activities to appease their unending need for entertainment. It seems sadly ironic that I shoo them away in order to write about parenting. Am I really loving my children? Or perhaps I shouldn't try to be available for their every need and whim.

There is probably not a day that goes by when I don't question my success as a mother, much less as a Catholic mom. By "Catholic mom" I simply mean a mother who in parenting her children draws on and is guided by her Christ-centered, sacramentally rich Catholic faith. There are days when I allow myself to be so discouraged by my current circumstances that I forget about the wisdom at my disposal. I believe this is precisely what the devil wants—for me to forget about God's grace that is available to me.

Thank goodness, God has been merciful by blessing me with the role of motherhood. Having five children spread out over eleven years has given me much time to stumble and fall before finding a groove in my effort to incorporate my Catholic spirituality into my vocation. No matter how weak or strong I've been in my faith on any given day, I know that God has always been there for me. He grants me peace whenever I commit myself to enduring the difficulties of being a mom, and he allows me to experience the pains of going off the mental deep end whenever I forget to turn to him for help.

Learning to Die to Myself

My first act in accepting my role as mother was simply agreeing to become a mother in the first place. After I married Greg, I loved my new role as wife as well as my independence as a working woman. Being a mom seemed like the unappealing option.

Thank goodness, I went only about a year into my marriage with that selfish mind-set. For some reason the idea of having a baby suddenly seemed intoxicating. Both Greg and I thought it would be cool to make a miniature version of us, so we decided to give it a go. I clearly had a lot to learn as a mom, but we all start somewhere, right?

It was during my pregnancy that I found myself yearning for a deeper connection with God again, but it would not be realized just yet. There would be more lessons for me to learn and more ways I would have to die to myself first.

When Greg and I were blessed with our first son, Sam, back in 1997, we made a bold decision that would put our faith to the test. We knew we wanted to uphold our parents' example of having Mom stay home from work in order to raise our new baby, but doing so would require help from God. After much discernment and prayer as a couple, we decided to jump off this cliff and completely trust that God would catch us before we crashed at the bottom. Before my sixth week of maternity leave came to an end, God answered our prayers and opened up a new door for Greg: a new job with better pay and benefits.

Whatever fantasies I had about the simple life of staying home with a baby (including leisurely strolls through parks with a perfectly behaved child) were quickly dashed. After about six months of round-the-clock care of our high-energy son, I was convinced that being a stay-at-home mom was infinitely harder than any stressful office job I'd had in the past. Adding to the struggle was the sense that my new role as mom was not "contributing to the family" because it didn't carry any monetary value. I actually harbored guilt for a long time, thinking that I was leaving the entire burden of providing for the family to Greg. What kind of wife was I? Where was the financial worth in all those diaper changes and sleepless nights?

Eighteen months later our second son, Walter, was born. But even with this tremendous blessing, I struggled to embrace my vocation as mother. Yes, I loved my two beautiful boys, but I also felt like a perpetual misfit in this role of mom.

I was hardly drawing on the wisdom of our faith to guide me in my understanding of what having children really meant. I was too spiritually immature to understand the meaning of love, sacrifice, and vocation.

Two years later our third son, Benjamin, was born. In his infinite mercy God had blessed me with a new attitude toward relying on him and trusting in him with my fertility. I started to embrace my mothering identity more than ever. I had opted to have an all-natural labor and delivery for the first time, to prove to myself that I could do it without fear. That experience must have made quite the impression on me, because within five minutes of Ben's birth, I knew I wanted another baby. Ben's sweet and tender disposition was a bit intoxicating to me, and I began to see children through a different lens—a holier lens—as pure blessings from God. I just had to learn to get myself out of the way, to trust God more and to worry less.

The Floor Is Not So Bad

Since becoming a mom I've done my fair share of off-the-wall things for my kids' sake. From catching bodily fluids with my bare hands to performing hand-puppet shows while driving a minivan, the checkered list seems infinite. But one simple act that I really didn't give much credit to was getting down on the floor to play with them.

I suppose it was for selfish reasons, like personal comfort, that I lacked motivation for doing this. The truth was, I didn't really like getting down on the hard floor where they were. Maintaining a clean house or spending a few hours on office work always seemed like a better idea than being sucked into their vortex of child's play all over my kitchen floor.

Over time I realized that I was actually doing the kids a bit of a disservice. For the more I remained above them, the more I perpetuated a kind of disconnect with them. What I thought was an unnecessary way of playing with them actually proved to be very important.

Getting down on their level gave me a chance to show a different kind of love to my kids—a love that said you matter to me, a love that said I love being with you, a love that put their needs ahead of my own, a love that helped me understand just what they were going through. The more I was able to understand their plight, the more I was able to be compassionate and loving toward them during their challenging times. All of this was made possible by my willingness to lie down next to them while they played with their train sets.

The Art of Storytelling

When I look back, I can see how God equipped me for my motherhood role in several ways. Since every mother is different and every child she has is different, it's logical to assume that the equipment God gives us will also be different. One of the gifts God has equipped me with is a good storytelling voice. There are plenty of times when I've wished he would have blessed me with good home-decorating skills, but alas, I digress.

One of my fondest memories from my childhood is of listening to my father make up adventurous bedtime stories for my brother and me. Dad possessed an uncanny ability to draw me into the heart-stopping adventures of his creative imagination. It was all in the way he used his voice. He truly was and still is a homespun master storyteller. He left a powerful impression on me.

I guess I inherited his knack. I am not anywhere as good as some of the famous American storytellers, but I can hold my own.

When God blesses us with a talent, he hopes we actually use it for his glory. Over the years I have learned to appreciate what I've been given and to use my voice to my mothering advantage.

One particular effort was to try to inspire the kids with heartfelt explanations about how to pray. To that end I shared with them, in the most compelling voice I could muster, some amazing stories about the saints. I prayed the rosary aloud for them in the most vibrant way I could. I put excitement in the way I explained the sacraments of our faith and into my explanations as to what it means to be Catholic. And the most amazing thing happened. I discovered that our kids were retaining a lot of what I was saying. Like a gardener sowing seeds, a mother can, by her words, sow seeds of love in the hearts of her children.

Do I always say the right things? No. There have been plenty of times when out of laziness I allowed my fair share of teachable moments to fall by the wayside. I know full well that I fall short of the glory of God (see Romans 3:23). But the important thing that I remember is to keep getting back up after I stumble, to keep leaning on him and using my God-given talents to help me make it through another day as the best mom I can be for my kids.

The Art of Listening

Being a mom has surely taught me some pretty valuable lessons that I've been able to directly apply to my relationship with Christ. But just when I thought I knew what I was doing, my children revealed yet another weakness in me that required strengthening: my ability to *listen* to them.

When they were little this was not a problem. I craved to hear them say their first word, which would of course be *Mama*. However, as their vocabulary grew along with their love of using it, my ability to listen to it all became strained, to say the least.

I sometimes chose the effortless route of listening to them with half an ear. Taking an interest in what they had to say was a sacrificial act that sometimes required more than I had to give, especially when I was tired. Only with God's help could I be the active listener that I knew I needed to be for the five children that he gave me to raise. This was an area where I knew I would have to seek special graces.

My biggest motivation to be the active listener to my kids is that God is an active listener to me. Since he has no problem allowing me to ramble on in my prayers before finally reaching my point, the least I could do is give my children the same gentle courtesy. The truth is, it's challenging for me to smile and listen my way through infinite stories of cool superheroes or to show expressions of compassion during the "He hit me" sagas. But by doing so, I know I'm affirming my children as individuals. I'm helping them find their own voices in this world and giving them the respect that they deserve.

For God's Sake

My journey to be the best mom I can be is far from over. I expect to fall several more times before it's done. But one thing is for sure: Raising these Willits kids has helped me in my own quest for holiness. By their steady revelations of my faults and weaknesses, they give me a fighting chance to grow.

My kids definitely made a mom out of me.

Now, if I were to think I could make myself into the perfect mom, I'd be a fool. I would quickly get stretched to gossamer threads before

I knew what hit me. Yet with God's grace, I make it day by day. For encouragement I often cite Matthew 19:26, "But Jesus looked at them and said to them: 'With men this is impossible but with God all things are possible,'" followed by my own personal mantra, "Without him I'm a miserable wreck."

By being faithful to the sacraments of marriage, reconciliation, Eucharist, confirmation, and baptism, I stay close to God. And when I stay close to God, I receive special graces that fuel my ability to be a good mother, to be a good wife, and to be a good steward of the talents God has blessed me with. When I remain faithful to him and obedient to his commands of love, I can rely on him to take care of things that I cannot.

There is only so much I can do as a human mother. The rest of my energies must be spent clinging to my faith daily, with bulldog tenacity, during good times and bad. If my children see anything in me, I want them to see a woman who is devoted to her faith and to serving others. Not a woman who cleans the house all the time (although cleanliness is important to me), nor a woman who spends all her spare time cooking and shopping and doing the budget (although that is important to me too), but a woman who attempts to serve the needs of all people for the love of God. If I can keep that up, with God's help, then I'll be that good mother that I always hoped I would be.

chapter seven

WHAT'S IT LIKE TO BE A GOOD CATHOLIC DAD?

Greg's Simple Rules for Awesome Dadness | *Greg*

The difference between the father I am now and the father I was as we were waiting for the birth of our first son couldn't be greater. It's more than just night-and-day different. I may as well have been a Little League pitcher tossed into the ninth inning of Game 7 of the World Series.

I'd read whatever I could about being a good dad, but the truth is that you can't really read your way into parenting. It's something that you have to experience and screw up, knowing that giving up is never an option. You must have a constant desire and commitment to improve, even though you'll always be deficient for the task.

There are some things I've gotten better at over the years. I wish there were some way I could have known these things years ago. If I could jump into a time-traveling DeLorean, go back to 1997, and walk up to my twenty-seven-year-old self as he was eating really bad hospital food just hours before his son was born, I could give myself a few pointers on how to be a good dad. It would be somewhat like the Boy Scout oath.

"A good dad is thrifty, resourceful, kind, loving, and goofy."

But the truth is, all these years of parenting later, I'm still figuring out what it means to be a good dad. And I imagine my own dad, now in his seventies, might sometimes ask himself if he's figured it out yet. For there is no Dad oath that could fully provide what it takes to raise good kids.

But there is one rule that I follow, and I believe it's the most important one. I believe all other rules flow from it, and everything else comes together when I remember to actually adhere to its simple premise.

So what's the rule? I'll get to that in a minute.

I recently had a candid conversation with our oldest son, who was thirteen at the time.

I told him I sometimes feel like a failure as a father.

I'm not sure if that was a stupid or a smart thing to admit to our teenage son. Would he use that statement against me someday? Would he no longer respect me as the predominant male figure in his life?

I tend to be overly honest, and that sometimes gets me into trouble. I tend to be overly honest, and that sometimes gets me into trouble. I tend to say to the people closest to me what's on my mind, and on that particular day I did feel a bit like a failure. Why?

Because I didn't seem to be following my simple rules of being a dad. And the rules are:

> Do whatever you can to get to heaven.
> Then do whatever you can to help get your wife to heaven.
> And then do whatever you can to help get your kids to heaven.
> And then if you can help anyone else get to heaven, that's just gravy.

I take these rules seriously, and they manifest themselves in many ways in my life.

Where's That Compass?

When we go on family road trips, I'm always the driver. In fact, after we got married, somehow it was silently implied that if both Jennifer and I were in the car, I'd be the one driving. It's not a sexist thing; it's just how it turned out. In fact, I'm not even sure I've been in a car with my wife in the past year when she's been driving. I pretty much have to have my gall bladder taken out before my wife gives up the passenger seat.

When it comes to getting our kids and my wife and myself to heaven, I feel that same responsibility of driving the van. I know how to get where we're going, and I've just got to make sure we all get there and that I don't accidentally leave anyone behind at a gas station along the way.

Now, let's go back to that conversation I recently had with my son Sam. Why did I feel like a failure? Because I stumble a lot, and I veer off the road, and sometimes I let my pride get in the way and don't stop to ask for directions and realign myself when I get lost.

And in our family, when I get knocked off course, there's a pileup.

When I lose my temper or let a not-so-appropriate word come flying out of my mouth, or if I spend too much time surfing the 'net or watching television instead of praying or leading the family in prayer, then it's not too long before our boys start shouting at each other more or my wife gets more prone to anger. Or we all find ourselves going days on end with only a half-sincere thanks to God before dinner.

A good dad is a compass. It's my job to stay directed and to set the example. When I look at the development of faith in our family, a very clear thread shows. Whenever I, as the father, lead the way in a spiritual endeavor, the family will follow and will blossom, and our individual and collective relationships with Christ will be strengthened.

And when I don't do that, I often feel like a failure.

That's not to say that Jennifer doesn't set an example or initiate prayer and other devotions. But it's different. And this chapter is not about being a good Catholic mom. That was the last chapter.

First Love

To be a good dad really doesn't require as much as we sometimes are led to believe.

My dad didn't take me to many sporting events, pack meetings, or amusement parks. He didn't buy me a lot of stuff either. Sure, we did things on occasion, and I always got presents for special occasions, but my dad didn't find it necessary to buy me stuff or to constantly fill my life with experiences. Those things just happened naturally.

What my dad did do, however, was love my mother. He'd bring her flowers when he didn't have to. He'd take her to dinner in the middle of the week. He'd take us to work with him on Saturday mornings to give my mom a break. He tried to be a spiritual leader in our household. He was there when he was needed. No huge things, just simple acts of love.

To me that's the greatest thing that my dad ever did. He modeled a good father by being a good husband. Because, naturally, when mom is taken care of, the children will be as well. That may sound sexist, but I don't mean it to be at all.

The truth is, the relationship that our kids have with their mother is far different from the one they have with me. With their mom there's a greater tenderness, more compassion, more kindness. With me there's more focus on diligence and persistence. They get a little from both of us, and hopefully that will pay off in the end.

To me a good father is one who tries to place his wife before himself. (If you think about it, that also defines everything Christ did for us.)

If I do all I can to make my wife feel complete, to take part of the stress off her shoulders, everything seems to be better, not only in our marriage but in our entire family. Our children are happier when mom is happier. My spiritual relationship with God seems to be better when mom's spiritual relationship with God is strong.

I stumble the most as a parent when I put myself before Jennifer. I forget that part of my task is to pray for her, to actively love her, and to help her get to heaven.

When it's easier to sleep through the sound of a crying baby instead of taking my turn, to ignore the dirty toilet instead of cleaning it, to move the shirts from the bed to the chair instead of putting them on hangers—those are times when I start to feel distant from my wife. And when I start to feel distant from her, I start to feel distant from my kids.

But when I fight to make little sacrifices, elevate my wife in our family, and remember to be a spiritual example, everything seems more perfectly aligned. In simple actions I can show Jennifer my love in tangible ways. And that love flows through our children and through our whole house and back to me, giving me even more desire to do even more for her.

My siblings and I all turned out somewhat OK. I trust our kids will too if I follow my father's example.

So you want to be a good Catholic dad? Love your wife more.

chapter eight

CATHOLIC LIFE IS EUCHARISTIC

Source and Summit | *Greg*

By the time I got married, I had lived in six states and ten homes. I'd been a regular parishioner in at least eight different parishes and had attended Mass at more churches in more cities and towns than I can easily recall.

And one thing I loved was that no matter where I went, Mass was pretty much the same. I knew the responses I was supposed to say; I knew when to sit, stand, or kneel. I knew we'd be hearing an Old Testament reading, one from the New Testament, a psalm, and a Gospel reading.

I was a cradle Catholic, and I knew the routine.

One tradition that I wish I had the opportunity to avail myself of during my formative years was the practice of prayerfully adoring our eucharistic Lord outside of Mass, a practice known as eucharistic adoration. Either I didn't get the memo about it or perhaps the parishes I had attended over the years were not in a position to offer it, but whatever the reason, I did not realize there were other opportunities to commune with our Lord outside of the celebration of Mass.

That being said, for the nearly thirty years of my cradle-Catholic life, my only experience with communing with the Eucharist was in the context of Mass. But like the dutiful cradle Catholic that I was, whenever I received the eucharistic host to the words "Body of

Christ," I quickly responded with the obligatory "Amen," ate the host, and crossed myself but had absolutely no understanding of the deep mystery that had just occurred.

Those thousands of Amens I said over the years were supposed to be affirmations that I truly believed that that little piece of bread and that tiny sip of wine were the body, blood, soul, and divinity of our Lord Jesus Christ. But because of my ignorance and lack of catechesis on this most important subject, I was saying Amen, as in "Yes, I believe," when I didn't have a clue.

Perhaps because I grew up in the seeming spiritual void of the 1970s and 1980s, I have no recollection of any teaching about the real presence of Jesus Christ in the Eucharist.

No one ever encouraged me to read and study John 6 or *Lumen Gentium* 11, which teaches that the Eucharist is the source and summit of our faith. And quite honestly, that ticks me off.

Now, that's not to say that growing up I didn't have the opportunity to know many wonderful priests and religious. From all the parishes I attended, I most certainly have known my fair share of dedicated priests and sisters. But sadly, none of them ever adequately explained the absolute reality of Christ's presence in the Eucharist.

From talking to countless people on our radio program who grew up at the same time as I did, I know for a fact that I'm not the only Catholic (or lapsed Catholic) who experienced the same spiritual void.

It honestly doesn't surprise me when I meet a baptized Catholic from my generation who no longer practices the faith.

I'm absolutely certain that if we start doing more to help people understand the Eucharist, the Church and our personal faith will flourish as we've never seen before.

And it's my goal as a parent to make sure our kids know that every time they say "Amen" at Communion, they know the miracle they are partaking of.

RCIA Wasn't Enough | *Jennifer*

From the time of my childhood up to my young adult life, my relationship with Jesus Christ was defined by my experiences with an obscure church that was once known as the Worldwide Church of God. In this faith practice God was vigorously preached about and vigorously obeyed by Old Testament standards. In fact, we heard the name *God* more than we did the name *Jesus Christ*. God was the heavenly Father, whom we talked about and obeyed strictly.

As recently as the 1980s, I was observing the holy days of the Jewish faith—the Sabbath (defined as the period from Friday night sundown to Saturday night sundown), the Day of Atonement, the Feast of Tabernacles, the Feast of Unleavened Bread, the Feast of Trumpets, and so on. But you wouldn't find any mention of Easter or Christmas on this church's calendar. Those were considered pagan rituals to be avoided.

There was little tradition in this nondenominational church and certainly no weekly communion. Not only was the church very anti-Catholic, but it also railed against standard Protestant tradition and many societal norms. This made for a rough experience for me in public school.

I mention this only to illustrate my spiritual roots in terms of understanding who Jesus Christ was and how I was to have a relationship with him. Because I clearly didn't have a strong foundation in Jesus, it was very easy for me to walk away from what I thought church was.

By the time I met Greg in 1994, I was spiritually empty and misguided, living only for myself, with God nothing more than a hazy memory in my mind. I'm amazed that Greg still wanted to marry me, knowing how non-Catholic and even nonreligious I was back then.

After we'd been married nearly three years and our first son was a year old, a greater desire for God began to stir within me. I experienced a spiritual hunger that was impossible to ignore, an undeniable tugging at my heart. I knew that God wanted me back.

But I had to get to know him all over again.

In December 1998, I enrolled in an RCIA (Rite of Christian Initiation of Adults) class. Though the classes had been in session several months already, I was quickly assigned a sponsor and welcomed into the fold with open arms. I had no problems with anything I heard in the class; everything made perfect sense. Scripture came alive. I found myself getting rather excited about how easy it was for me to accept the teachings that just months before I had considered to be pagan beliefs!

I anticipated receiving the Eucharist as my final reward on entering into full communion with the Catholic Church. It was easy for me to accept the truth that the Eucharist is the body, blood, soul, and divinity of our Lord Jesus Christ—with my head. It was another thing entirely to understand the teaching with my heart.

I was like an eager bride approaching my wedding for the romance of it rather than with a genuine understanding of the nature of marriage. I understood the general concept of the Eucharist, but I didn't really understand what I'd receive. How could placing the Eucharist in my mouth be the very pinnacle of my faith? How is this small manna-like Host equivalent to our Lord and our heavenly Creator?

Eventually I would learn that these questions can be answered only with the eyes of faith.

Jesus Is Coming | *Greg*

Our third son, Ben, was just two months old, and our other boys were four and two. The idea of bringing them to an event with fifteen thousand people and expecting them to be quiet and cooperative for eight hours was just ridiculous. Yet I couldn't get it out of my head.

The Eucharistic Congress had been meeting in Atlanta for a few years when, in 2002, Jennifer and I found ourselves on fire for our faith as never before. God was opening our eyes to the wonders of the Eucharist in ways I had never imagined. I was reading John 6 over and over again: "So Jesus said to them, 'Truly, truly, I say to you, unless you eat the flesh of the Son of man and drink his blood, you have no life in you; he who eats my flesh and drinks my blood has eternal life, and I will raise him up at the last day'" (John 6:53–54). I'd read this before and heard it proclaimed at Mass, but now when I read these passages, I would shake my head in disbelief: "How could I have missed this all along?"

I am fortunate to belong to a parish that offers monthly eucharistic adoration. For the previous few months, I'd spent several hours in the chapel, trying to overcome a lifetime of ignorance and discerning whether I really believed the teaching of the Church in this respect.

I'd sit silently, staring at the monstrance and the Eucharist within, continually asking in disbelief, "Are you really there, God? Is that really you? How is it that I've gone nearly thirty years without knowing that the Church teaches that the bread and wine truly become *you*? And that the Bible backs it up?"

The insatiable desire to better understand this mystery became my primary focus. When I'd receive the Eucharist, I was saying "Amen" with more awareness than I'd ever had before. But still a twinge of doubt remained.

My search was drawing me to uncharacteristic actions. On that early Saturday morning in 2002, I was walking circles around our living room, calming my new son and constantly returning to the kitchen counter, where the local Catholic newspaper was open. Directions to the event beckoned me to get the family in the van and just go. But just above the map was the warning "Parking is limited. Be sure to arrive early to get a spot."

Those were the words making me hesitate that morning. (Just a word to anyone in charge of planning an event: Never tell anyone parking is limited. That's a surefire way to make people seriously consider skipping it.)

But the desire to more fully experience the Eucharist was too much to resist.

Finally I went to Jennifer and told her, "Let's just go for it."

We got on the road, still feeling somewhat frightened, worried, and unprepared for what lay ahead.

There was a children's track for our oldest son, and day care was also available. We rushed our two oldest children to these separate locations. Then, holding our son Ben, we joined the throngs of people making their way down a long narrow hall to the main event.

"Why are we here, Lord?" I kept praying. "What is so important that I couldn't stop thinking about this event?"

I don't particularly like crowded areas. Everything around me became muted and fuzzy. Was I having some sort of panic attack?

Jennifer and I both worried about the fact that we had already missed the first speakers of the day. And we had left our two young boys in the care of strangers. Yet we pushed our way along the edge of the crowd, numbness going from my head to my arms and down to my feet.

We heard the sound of bells ringing, faint but growing louder. Then we heard voices.

"Jesus is coming," people were saying. "Jesus is coming."

All around us people whispered to each other, "Jesus is coming."

To our left and right people were dropping to their knees. And from the end of the hall we saw a procession coming toward us. Acolytes in white robes holding candles walked before the archbishop, who held an enormous gold monstrance in his cloth-covered hands, the consecrated host in its center.

"Jesus is coming. Jesus is coming."

My wife and I dropped to our knees as well. I clutched Ben more tightly in my arms and, as the bells grew louder and the voices grew silent, I stared at what looked like an enormous piece of bread in the monstrance. And I knew with every fiber of my being that it was in fact Jesus Christ, truly present, who has "the words of eternal life" (John 6:68) and promises that whoever "believes in him should have eternal life" (John 6:40). I knew beyond a doubt that "this is the bread which comes down from heaven, that a man may eat of it and not die" (John 6:50) and that "if any one eats of this bread, he will live for ever; and the bread which I shall give for the life of the world is my flesh" (John 6:51). I knew that "this is the bread which came down from heaven" (John 6:58).

I stared at that Host, and tears flooded my eyes. For the first time in my life, I fully believed.

Keeping It Real | *Jennifer*

Sad to say, there were times I received the Eucharist, sat back down in the pew, and thought to myself, "Did I just receive?"

Moments like that could leave me feeling spiritually weak, embarrassed, and undeserving. The devil scored by making me feel like an idiot at Mass.

"Wonderful," I'd think. "I can't even receive the Eucharist right!"

But the reality is, I *did* receive Jesus in the Eucharist, whether my mental faculties were present or not. Nothing can alter that fact. My mind might have drifted, but my physical presence was there, as was our Lord's.

Fr. Jay Finelli, a priest in Rhode Island and a personal friend, reminded me that if we receive the Eucharist only when we are in a perfect mental state, we would not receive very often at all. And the moment I return to my senses and reconnect with the Lord in prayers of thanksgiving for that precious gift he gave me, I "score" spiritually.

This mental struggle reminds me that we're living in a constant spiritual battle. We can't pretend we're not targets for evil forces.

One of the best ways to keep the Eucharist vibrant and real in our spiritual life is to understand that he is in fact *real* in the first place. If you see the Eucharist only as a small white circular host and nothing more, then you miss out on a deeper truth and reality.

Living in the archdiocese of Atlanta, I have been blessed to attend the annual Eucharistic Congress several times. Part of the itinerary for this event, held around the Feast of Corpus Christi in early summer, is a healing service on the Friday evening before the main Saturday event.

Not having much experience with Catholic healing services, I attended one year when Sr. Briege McKenna was leading it. Sr. Briege, a member of the Sisters of St. Clare, is known for her worldwide ministry to priests and for her healing ministry. Her own healing from crippling arthritis is recounted in her book *Miracles Do Happen*.[11]

That night Sr. Briege was my gentle reminder that Jesus is fully present and alive to us here and now. Over and over she stated in her beautiful Irish brogue that Jesus is here. *Jesus is here.* If only we'd see him with our eyes of faith!

This healing service was like nothing I'd attended before. I had thought it would appeal only to the physically needy, but I quickly realized that we are all in need of healing. Jesus was right there in front of us, physically present in the Eucharist, ready to do the work. And the beauty of this is that we need not attend an occasional healing service to receive this healing power. Every time we go to Mass, we are in fact receiving it. What a powerful lesson I learned that day.

Keep It Simple | *Greg*

When I leave the house to go to eucharistic adoration, I often walk out with my Bible, a notebook, and five other books, just in case the Holy Spirit prompts me in unexpected directions. Most often those books sit next to me, completely untouched, as I do nothing more than stare at the Blessed Sacrament in the monstrance.

On other occasions my notebook is my best friend, as I write letter after letter to Jesus with prose much clearer than the ramblings in my brain.

Other times I might see a priest walk through the chapel, and I'm reminded that I haven't gone to confession in a while. So I say a prayer, asking the Holy Spirit to help me recall my sinful behavior. I might even track the priest down later to receive the sacrament of reconciliation before going home.

---

11. Briege McKenna with Henry Libersat, *Miracles Do Happen* (Ann Arbor, Mich.: Charis, 1996).

I've found the best thing to avoid at adoration is overcomplicating it. Just be there.

Walk in, genuflect on both knees, bow before our Lord, thank him for the opportunity, thank him for the understanding of his real presence, and then sit or kneel and simply wait for the Holy Spirit to move. While it may look as if I'm just sitting idle, I've found that, in those moments of stillness, the Lord does the most amazing things in my life. He might move me to pick up my Bible, or he might move me to pray for my enemies. If there is ever a time to try to follow the quiet whisperings of the Holy Spirit, it is in the real presence of Our Lord Jesus Christ.

There are times when I walk out after an hour and feel disappointed or distracted. That's OK. That happens in relationships, and spending time in adoration is simply a way of building and strengthening a relationship with Jesus. And no relationship is ever complete. It's an ongoing, changing, growing, strengthening, exciting, unending dance between persons.

As Bl. John Paul II wrote:

> The Church and the world have a great need of eucharistic worship. Jesus awaits us in this sacrament of love. Let us not refuse the time to go to meet him in adoration, in contemplation full of faith, and open to making amends for the serious offenses and crimes of the world. Let our adoration never cease. (*Dominicae Cenae*, 3, quoted in *CCC*, 1380).

Introducing the Kids to Jesus | *Jennifer*

What about my children? How can I help them develop the kind of closeness to and understanding of the real presence that I've grown to know over the past ten years?

Should I haul our rowdy gaggle of boys into this serene and holy setting where you can hear a pin drop?

I struggled with this for a while. I know how loud our kids can be! I didn't have the heart to disrupt the other parishioners who took precious time out of their days to be there so as to steep themselves in prayer.

"Let the children come to me."

"I hear you, Lord," I'd respond. "But they're so loud!"

"Let the children come to me."

"All right, you win."

So one night I decided to take the direct approach with our boys.

"Who wants to go see Jesus tonight?" That got their attention. "I'm going to see him at church. Do you want to come with me?" I asked.

"Sure! I'll come," was the unanimous reply.

It didn't matter to me that they were more concerned with getting out of the house than with actually bonding with Jesus. At least they were coming.

Knowing that I had a captive audience in the van on the way to church, I explained the tradition of eucharistic adoration with the best age-appropriate explanation I could muster. The kids nodded in agreement. Sure, they understood what we were about to do.

"So far, so good," I thought.

I further explained, in my purposefully light and happy tone of voice, that since we were going to be sitting there before our Lord in the monstrance, it would be very appropriate to spend some time just talking to him in the form of spontaneous or conversational prayer.

"Just share your hurts, your joys, anything you want," I told the van full of boys. "This is your time to get to know him a little better. If you want to pray traditional prayers like the rosary, that would be equally wonderful."

I looked in the rearview mirror and saw several blank expressions.

"After you've spent some time talking with Jesus, you can read your Bibles or other spiritual books while you are in his presence. If you want to draw religious artwork quietly, you can do that as well."

There. Something for all ages. This should go well.

We entered into the chapel slowly but purposefully. I led the way, showing the children that every step we take here is special—no heavy and absentminded moves. I modeled the practice of genuflecting before entering the pew, and like obedient little ducklings following their mama duck, they copied me. We settled into our pew of choice, and the boys followed my example of kneeling down for a time of prayer.

I quickly surmised that I had underestimated just how quiet the silence is in our parish's chapel space. I was nervous that every breath my kids made would be considered disruptive by a parishioner praying nearby. My stress slowly rose. My prayers were suddenly all about begging our Lord to keep my kids quiet and respectful of others' need for prayer.

Whoosh. Whoosh. Scraaapppe. Whoosh.

Without even opening my eyes, I knew that telltale sound. It was the sound of pages of a book being vigorously flipped by the slightly uncoordinated hands of a child.

My child.

Page-flipping had never sounded so loud and distracting as it did in that moment. The acoustics of the chapel somehow magnified that whooshing to an uncomfortably high volume.

I leaned over and gently whispered into the little ears of our youngest two sons, Ben and Tommy, to *please* turn the pages more quietly. The slower page-flipping lasted for about two minutes. Then the high-decibel sounds were back.

Whoosh. Whoosh. Scraaapppe. Whoosh.

"Let the children come to me."

"I know, I know! But the noise of the pages is so loud!"

"Let the children come to me."

"All right, Lord! All right!"

I'm sure my overactive imagination increased the actual sounds of pages turning; God was not bothered in the slightest. I had brought my children to him.

The boys surprised me with their ability to sit still and refrain from talking. In fact, aside from the vigorous turning of pages, they were silent and respectful. When after a good twenty minutes in adoration I gave them the cue that we were leaving, they quietly followed me out. I was quick to thank them for their reverent behavior. They surprised me by saying they enjoyed their quiet time with Jesus.

Music to this mother's ears.

I wish I could say that my children always accompany me to eucharistic adoration, but they do not. I offer them the opportunity, and sometimes all or a couple of them will join me.

And sometimes no one does. But that's OK.

I will continue to offer it to them freely. I know that I am exposing them to something beautiful. Little holy seeds have been planted in them. I will now allow them to germinate. Jesus is there for us always.

The more I frequent eucharistic adoration, the more I feel a bond growing between the Lord and me. There are times when I sit in the peaceful environment of our parish chapel and find it therapeutic in nature. At other times the Lord and I have a productive brainstorming session about an important situation in my life.

Going to adoration gives me an opportunity to hang out with Jesus. I'm getting to know him in the nitty-gritty within the confines of prayer, just as people in the flesh get to know one another in the physical life. I get to engage in a real and vibrant dialogue that brings all of me to him. It helps me grow in my understanding of his presence at every moment of my life.

This is what I want our children to ultimately learn: There is power and fruit to be harvested from the simplicity of eucharistic adoration.

So I encourage you to find a chapel where you can adore the body of Christ.

Do it as often as you can. And let the children come.

chapter nine
SQUEAKY CLEAN

Predisposed to Idiocy | *Greg*

One thing I love about the *Catechism of the Catholic Church* is that it often has explanations for my idiocy.

For example, in section 418 the *Catechism* says that we are indeed predisposed to sin: "As a result of original sin, human nature is weakened in its powers; subject to ignorance, suffering, and the domination of death; and inclined to sin (This inclination is called 'concupiscence')."

While that doesn't let us off the hook for our sins, it certainly is helpful to know that if we are predisposed to sin, God has also provided a way for us to seek forgiveness, become strengthened in grace, and move forward.

A Flowing River of Grace | *Jennifer*

While many of our common imperfections equate to venial sins (sins that do not sever our relationship with God), if left unchecked they can lead to mortal sins (the sins that are serious and destructive of our relationship with God).

The *Catechism* tells us that "venial sin weakens charity; it manifests a disordered affection for created goods; it impedes the soul's progress in the exercise of the virtues and the practice of the moral good; it merits temporal punishment" (*CCC*, 1863).

83

In other words, venial sins have the ability to weaken our souls. Mortal sins, on the other hand, have the ability to kill it.

Kill it?

Yep. Mortal sins are *that* serious. That's why they're called "mortal."

I like to draw the analogy between grace and water. Grace—God's unmerited favor—flows to us like a spiritual river. If there are no obstacles in this flow of life-giving grace, the full measure of grace will reach our soul.

A venial sin is like a pebble tossed into the middle of our river. One pebble alone will not create much of a problem, if any, to this flow of grace.

But we don't want too many pebbles there. Otherwise the grace that can reach us will be reduced to a mere trickle. Even though we might not feel it, our soul is greatly weakened, which leads to another harsh reality: Mortal sin is now much easier to commit.

So that's why I try to go to confession regularly, to get rid even of little pebbles.

I Don't Need to Confess My Sins to No Priest! | *Greg*

Like a lot of people who grew up post–Vatican II, my family did not experience going to confession as a part of our regular spiritual life. The sacrament seemed like an outdated practice to be avoided as much as possible.

Yet confession is one of the iconic aspects of Catholicism. Even non-Catholics know from movies and television that the first thing you do when you walk into a confessional and shut the door is to make the Sign of the Cross and say, "Bless me, Father, for I have sinned."

How often do we take advantage of the sacrament?

A few years ago I was talking with a fellow parishioner after Mass, and he made a rather off-color comment. I jokingly told him, "Ah, you better go confess that one!"

This friend—a convert, a lector, well-known and well respected, who had married into a family that had been active in the parish since its inception decades before—took me off guard by responding, "I've never been to confession, and I'll never go. I don't need to tell a priest my sins."

Now, I have no idea how this man converted to Catholicism or received the Eucharist without first going to confession. His statement not only surprised me but made me sad. This friend and fellow parishioner had no idea what he was missing.

Something's in My Eye, but I Can't See What It Is | *Jennifer*

Ever since I completed my initiation into the Catholic Church at the Easter Vigil Mass of 1999, I have struggled with examining my conscience the way I perceive the Church wants me to. I understand the concept. I agree with the concept. I'm just terrible at it. At least that's how I feel.

Matthew 7:3–5 seems to echo in my thoughts when I try to sit down and examine my sins:

> Why do you see the speck that is in your brother's eye, but do not notice the log that is in your own eye? Or how can you say to your brother, 'Let me take the speck out of your eye,' when there is the log in your own eye? You hypocrite, first take the log out of your own eye, and then you will see clearly to take the speck out of your brother's eye.

I think of this passage so often because this is usually my problem.

I know I'm sinful, but I'm just terrible about remembering my sins when it comes time for confession. And unfortunately, I am quite good at pointing out the flaws of others. Why is this the case?

I wonder if anyone else suffers from this spiritual blindness. I rarely hear anyone admit to the condition. This can make me feel alone and discouraged. But then I wonder, is it some deep dark secret everyone is carrying around?

That Jesus talks about it makes me suspect that there are lots of people out there who deal with the same issue. So I want to encourage you to grab ahold of any wooden beam in your eye and remove it. After all, you deserve better than to go through life with a big chunk of wood in your face, right?

Bubble Trouble | *Greg*

Back in the 1970s there was a commercial for dishwashing soap in which someone standing over a sink full of bubbles pulled out a dish, rubbed a finger over its surface, and proclaimed, "It's squeaky clean!"

When our oldest son was about to make his first confession, I told him about that commercial.

I asked Sam to imagine that his soul was like a dish. Every time he sinned, it was as if someone had thrown a big spoonful of marinara sauce on the plate. Enough splotches on his plate would make the dish very unappealing and hard to handle.

I further explained that if you were to take that dish and set it under the flame of a broiler, eventually that marinara sauce would burn and smell. It would cling so intently that the plate would seem impossible to clean. And if you took the plate out of the broiler, it would be so hot that you couldn't touch it, and neither could anyone else. It would have to be separated from the other dishes and maybe even tossed out if not taken care of properly. The dish could be lost forever.

But if you washed the plate the right way, with the right soap and hot water, even the messiest, caked-on plate could get clean. And not just clean but squeaky clean! Let's be honest. Wouldn't you prefer a plate that was squeaky clean instead of just plain ol' regular clean?

Our souls, I explained to my son, we cake with sin after sin. If we let those sins sit too long, we might convince ourselves that there's no way our soul could ever get clean. And if we keep sinning over and over again—throwing marinara sauce on the plate time and again—it can seem impossible to grow in our faith as God would want us to. Our sins then may separate us from our loved ones, and they most definitely would separate us from God.

But if we take our sinful selves to confession, we can have confidence that God—the ultimate supernatural dishwashing detergent for humans—will forgive our sins and make our souls squeaky clean. No matter how long a sin has been resting on your soul, no matter how bad the sin might be, a priest, through the power of God, can absolve you of it if you confess it.

"If we confess our sins, he is faithful and just, and will forgive our sins and cleanse us from all unrighteousness" (1 John 1:9).

When one of our children walks out of the confessional, one of us, Jennifer or I, is often waiting for him. And we have a tradition of pinching his cheek and saying, "Squeak, squeak, squeak! You're squeaky clean!"

The children think we're insane, of course, but they get the point. They know that when they avail themselves of this loving, healing sacrament provided by Christ, they are cleansed from all unrighteousness. They become unified with Christ again, no longer separated from the clean dishes. They become a part of the community of believers once more. They become reconciled.

In John 20:21–23, Jesus tells his apostles, "As the Father has sent me, even so I send you.... Receive the Holy Spirit. If you forgive the sins of any, they are forgiven; if you retain the sins of any, they are retained."

Christ himself instituted this sacrament. Why would he have bothered to give his apostles this authority to forgive if it was not something that would benefit us and draw us closer to him?

God wants us to be squeaky clean, and he's given us the means of getting there. But if we don't get ourselves to the sink, the dishes won't be cleaned. Likewise, if we don't get ourselves to confession, our souls won't be either.

A Gift to Be Unwrapped | *Jennifer*

Jesus clearly knew that we, as flawed human beings, were going to need a way back into God's good graces, a way to wipe away the consequences of our sins of today. Even though Jesus died for our sins, we can still freely choose to reject God and end up in hell.

A priest once told me that my salvation is like a beautifully wrapped present that was given to me when Jesus died on the cross. However, this gift of salvation comes with two conditions:

First, I can hold on to this gift as long as I am living in a state of grace. But when I commit sin, I in essence reject God's love and throw the gift away.

Second, I don't get to open this gift completely until I die.

Don't you want to hold on to the gift of salvation? I surely do. But even with my good intentions, I find myself throwing the gift away on occasion because of my sins. Thanks to the sacrament of reconciliation, I can pick up the gift again.

The stakes may be high, but Christ is merciful. He makes it easy for us to come back to him, no matter how bad our imperfections and sins may be.

Free Grace | *Greg*

But what about those areas of our lives where we keep sinning the same sin over and over? What about those imperfections that we just can't seem to defeat? If you're struggling in some way in your life, as a parent or spouse or friend or child, perhaps there's something deeper that needs to be addressed. If we are to be the people God calls us to be, we need to do it his way. And it's really not that difficult.

For me one of the worst feelings is waiting in line to confess my sins.

But there's also no greater feeling than walking out of the confessional and knowing that my sins have been forgiven in a way that only God, in his infinite love and mercy and through the sacrifice of his Son, Jesus Christ, can forgive.

And here's the even better news: When I avail myself of frequent confession, God gives me the graces to overcome the weaknesses in my life.

You may have some irritating sinful behavior that seems like a borderline addiction, but when you seek God's forgiveness in the sacrament of confession, he rewards you with grace to overcome the sins that hold you down.

Again, in the *Catechism*, we read that "venial sin does not break the covenant with God. With God's grace it is humanly reparable" (*CCC*, 1863).

No matter how much time our sin-caked souls growing more soiled and hardened with venial sins, God can clean up the mess if we only ask him to do so. And furthermore, each time we go to confession, he gives us additional graces, in order to strengthen us against those sins that regularly hold us back from being the best Christian we can be, whether parent, spouse, friend, or child.

Sometimes we feel inadequate because we're not the best examples to our kids. We don't always model proper responses to situations. We may say, think, or do things that separate us from our families, friends, and God. But when we give our stumblings and failures and inadequacies to God, he can lead us to become perfect.

A Quick Exam | *Jennifer*

So far the best way I've found of seeing myself for who I am is to honestly answer some seriously probing questions through a typical examination of conscience. The trick for me has always been finding the right set of questions, ones that really resonate with the flaws I'm struggling with.

Over the years I have read through many different lists of questions based on the Ten Commandments or the Beatitudes.

What I have discovered is that there is not one perfect list of questions that works for my specific circumstances in life. Some self-examination questions seem overly tedious, while others seem too broad. Other questions seem to be out of sync with my current state in life. And, yes, others are spot-on.

Well, I'd like to make things really simple for you. Probably the most important questions you can ask yourself, no matter what state in life you find yourself in, are these:

> How today have you loved your Lord, your God, and how
> have you failed to love God?

How have you loved the people around you, and how have
   you failed to love them?
How have you loved yourself, and how have you failed to
   love yourself?

I think that if you stop for a moment and really meditate on these
three questions, you'll be amazed at some of the weaknesses you
discover about yourself and at areas where you have blatantly sinned.

On days when I'm feeling a bit lazy when trying to examine my
conscience, I like to joke around with Greg and just ask him what my
failings are! I know for a fact he'd be able to find some faults that he'd
like to see changed. Of course, he never tells me, because he knows
better than to fall for that trap.

chapter ten
FAMILY-ROSARY WRESTLING

Having a Family Spirituality | *Jennifer*

What does it mean to have a family spirituality? Perhaps another way of looking at this question is to simply ask, should we work on having a family spirituality? An individual spiritual life, certainly, but what about family spirituality?

Depending on what age you are and how large your family is, answers to that question will undoubtedly vary. I would hope that by the end of this chapter our Lord might have inspired you to see that a good family spirituality is indeed something to be sought after daily.

Before I share my thoughts on family spirituality more deeply, I want to clarify what I mean by *spirituality*, since this term can have many definitions. Simply put, spirituality, in and of itself, is our moral and religious nature. It is largely influenced by three main factors: our life experience in the world, our experience with our Lord, and our own free will. All three factors are unique to each of us and strongly dictate the direction that our moral and religious nature will take.

A Catholic family spirituality is the moral and religious way that a family strives to live in society while remaining loyal to the magisterium of the Catholic Church. In order for this family spirituality to be present and fruitful to the Church and society as a whole, it must involve the entire family as much as possible, not just the interior life of the parents.

If you were to take a spiritual snapshot of your family life right now, what would that picture reveal? Indeed, God sees this picture of us every day, but how often do we try to see it as God does?

Defining Spirituality | *Greg*

Though we hear the word *spirituality* quite frequently in our lives as Christians, it's surprisingly difficult to find a clear-cut answer as to what exactly it is. The *Catechism* does not include the word in its index. We do find in the *Catechism* this rather puzzling description:

> A distinct spirituality can also arise at the point of conver-
> gence of liturgical and theological currents, bearing witness
> to the integration of the faith into a particular human envi-
> ronment and its history. The different schools of Christian
> spirituality share in the living tradition of prayer and are
> essential guides for the faithful. In their rich diversity they
> are refractions of the one pure light of the Holy Spirit. (*CCC*,
> 2684)

What the heck does that mean?

How do I develop a spirituality when it's hard to get a proper defi-
nition of it? And furthermore, how do I develop a spirituality in the midst of screaming kids, pressing deadlines, an empty refrigerator, and a mess that the dog left on the carpet because no one bothered to let her out after she barked at the back door for ten minutes?

Again going to the *Catechism* index, we do find "Spirit: see Holy Spirit."

Suddenly it becomes obvious that our spirituality is our relationship and cooperation with the Holy Spirit. Simple enough.

But do we understand the Holy Spirit enough to have a relationship with him?

The *Catechism's* glossary describes the Holy Spirit as "the third divine Person of the Blessed Trinity, the personal love of Father and Son for each other. Also called the Paraclete (Advocate) and Spirit of Truth, the Holy Spirit is at work with the Father and the Son from the beginning to the completion of the divine plan for our salvation."

That's getting us closer to understanding, though it's still a little muddled. We're trying to understand how to have not only a personal, individual relationship with the Holy Spirit but also a relationship with him involving the whole family.

The key word to focus on in that definition is *love*. The Holy Spirit is "the personal love of the Father and Son for each other."

When we ask for the guidance of the Holy Spirit, or when we try to act in the Holy Spirit, we are called to act in a loving way, a way that mirrors the love that God the Father poured out onto Jesus the Son.

The Holy Spirit, in essence, is an outpouring of love, and the Spirit dwelling in us allows us to act in the love of Christ. Spirituality is our relationship with the Holy Spirit, the way we interact with the Holy Spirit, and the way the Holy Spirit compels us to interact with—and love—others.

The Holy Spirit presents us with a blessed opportunity to be like Christ, who poured himself out for us in love. With the help of the Holy Spirit, we can overcome our human frailties and pour ourselves out in love to others.

In a nutshell, our spirituality amounts to our allowing the Holy Spirit (again—the personal love of God the Father and Jesus Christ) to dwell within us and cooperating with him.

So how do we cooperate?

We cooperate both as individuals and as a collective family unit.

We cooperate through prayer. We cooperate by our love for others.

We cooperate when we take active steps to develop with the Holy Spirit a relationship that allows us to be more life-giving and love-giving and Spirit-driven.

Making an Impression | *Jennifer*
As I sought to understand our own family's spirituality, I realized that I would have to look back a little to see just *how* our life experiences have shaped the family spirituality thus far.

Once Greg and I made a commitment to work in ministry, we did our best to work in some capacity of evangelization for the Catholic Church. It all started with the formation of Rosary Army Corp back in 2003. Next we joined forces with Fr. Roderick Vonhögen from the Netherlands to start the Star Quest Production Network here in the United States. While pulling double duty with both international apostolates, Greg and I managed to find the time to produce a comedic video series known as *That Catholic Show*. And just when we were about to kick off a second series, we landed a new career hosting on the Catholic Channel a radio talk show known as *The Catholics Next Door with Greg and Jennifer Willits*. This was life in the Willits house.

Of course, these experiences in our career path brought with them tremendous potential to influence and encourage a rich family spirituality. But because none of us is perfect in Christ, we still manage to fumble around spiritually and make plenty of mistakes in our choices for our lives. Having a career in Catholic evangelization will not turn us into saints. Rather our determination to love as God loves, in every situation, urges us on toward sanctity.

For the most part, our ministry has had a positive effect on our family spirituality. For instance, our kids were able to witness firsthand the formation of Rosary Army and how it happily threatened to take over every inch of available space in our house! Rosaries were constantly being sorted and prepped for mailing, and the dining-room table and living-room floor were inevitably the best places to do it. Rosary storage bins were eventually lining the hallways and occupying our garage. But it wasn't just the physical presence of all the rosaries that made an impression on our kids' minds; it was what the rosaries led us to—praying with them.

The problem was, praying a family rosary was far easier in theory than it was in practice. This was especially true when our children were little. There were many family rosaries that left Greg and me feeling as if we had survived a wrestling match. Our two- and four-year-old boys thought it was great fun to jump around the living room while trying to lasso each other with the enormous supply of rosaries they had at their disposal. No matter how hard we tried to pray a reverent Hail Mary, these stressful conditions definitely took some serenity out of the moment.

There were times when uncontrollable and contagious giggles would erupt among the kids. One such occasion occurred after I asked who could tell me the name of the next sorrowful mystery. With all seriousness, our then six-year-old son, Tommy, confidently yelled out, "The scourging of the caterpillar!" We almost didn't recover.

No matter how imperfect the family rosary turned out to be, we knew it was well worth our effort. If praying a full rosary was too challenging for whatever reason, we would try to pray just a decade instead. The point was to come together as a family to pray together as one.

The rosary is one of the few prayers I know of that engages the mind, the body, and the soul. The mind meditates on the life of Jesus.

The body both holds the rosary and utters the words from the Gospel, while the soul receives grace. Even imperfect rosaries can help nurture a good family spirituality.

Foundations of Spirituality | *Greg*

The disciples asked Jesus, "Lord, teach us to pray" (Luke 11:1).

As modern-day disciples, we have an innate desire to grow closer to God. The desire for happiness, for something better in life, for a deepened understanding of our purpose in this world, is driven by a God-given desire to know God better.

Through prayer we can accomplish this, but for a deeper spirituality, one that goes below the surface, the Church has provided many tools. By acquainting ourselves with them, we allow the Spirit to work in and through us more.

In his book *Rediscover Catholicism*, Matthew Kelly identifies seven pillars of spirituality: reconciliation, contemplation, the Mass, the Bible, fasting, spiritual reading, and the rosary.[12]

I've come to realize that incorporating all these pillars into my life will require a lifetime of work. I, too, often allow the busyness of my day to interfere with the practice of those seven pillars.

Even if we were all able to work on all seven on a daily basis, we'd most likely approach them in different ways. Perhaps the best fast for you would be to fast from television for a day or two. Maybe the best spiritual reading would simply be the *Catechism*. What the Holy Spirit wants you to work on is between you and the Holy Spirit. What's important is to make sure you are taking active steps to constantly improve in those seven areas.

---

12. Matthew Kelly, *Rediscover Catholicism: A Spiritual Guide to Living With Passion and Purpose* (Cincinnati: Beacon, 2002).

A Work in Progress | *Jennifer*

Our family's spirituality is a work in progress. There will be victories and head-smacking embarrassments. But as long as we maintain our focus on Christ, stay close to him in the sacraments, and remain loyal to the teachings of our faith to the best of our abilities, we will be equipped to handle any challenge God wants to put before us.

Do we pray perfectly every day as a family? No. Do we try our best? Yes.

Do we read Scripture around the dinner table every night? Not always, but we do talk about and reference Scripture when it makes sense to.

Do I fill our family schedule with multiple charitable activities? Not at the moment, but we do encourage and try to foster an attitude of love and giving when possible.

I do my best, and I pray for continued strength to do just that every day. It's only by the grace of God that I can accomplish anything in this house. So why not tap into that grace as often as possible?

What Kind of Spirituality Are You Called To? | *Greg*

I'm big into lists. Colleagues regularly tease me because I tend to make a spreadsheet for just about everything.

If you want to develop a stronger individual spirituality as well as a more defined family spirituality, I recommend brainstorming all of the ways you'd like to grow closer to God. What are all of the forms of prayer that at some point have made you think, "I wish I did that more often"? Maybe it's praying the rosary. Maybe it's going to confession more often.

Write all of those things down.

Now, pray about those things. First pray about them on your own. Ask God what kind of spirituality he's calling you to. Then go through your list and mark the things you can realistically accomplish every day or at least do on a more regular basis. Perhaps your friend can pray three rosaries a day, and that's admirable, but keep in mind that you must find your own spirituality, and maybe that's not what God is calling you to right now.

Go back through the list, and of the things you marked for daily practice, ask if those are things you can also do with your family. If you want to go to confession every month or every two weeks, can you do that as a family as well? Mark that on the list then.

As for the things you didn't mark, don't discount them as unrealistic aspirations. Put those on a separate list, labeled "Items to Pray About From Time to Time." Regularly ask the Holy Spirit to help you do a spiritual checkup to make sure you're doing the right spiritual exercises in your life.

If spirituality is new to you, don't try to take on too much at first. If you decide tomorrow you'll do everything—read the Bible for fifteen minutes, read some other spiritual book for fifteen minutes, pray a rosary alone, pray another rosary with the family, take the family to daily Mass, and visit the sick on the way home—you'll probably burn out.

Take small steps, and allow the Holy Spirit to guide both you and your family in growing closer to him. If you want to start praying a family rosary, maybe start by praying an Our Father, a Hail Mary, and a Glory Be one day. The next day pray a decade, and eventually work your way up to a whole rosary.

Developing a spirituality for both you as well as your family is a challenge. Sometimes you'll feel as if you're wrestling with yourself, with God, with the devil, and with your children.

But with each struggle your spirituality will develop, both in your own soul and in your family. And with the help of the Holy Spirit, overcoming the challenges will strengthen you even more to pour love out to others as the Father did to the Son and as the Son did for each of us.

chapter eleven

THE FIRST TEACHERS

The Curriculum Crunch | *Jennifer*

The subject of educating our children is perhaps the single area in my life that causes me the most joy and the most frustration. Long have I wrestled with this beast. Long have I counted the victories and setbacks. Long have I wondered if I have successfully drawn on my faith as a source of guidance in the education of our children.

When our first son, Sam, was approaching the age of four, I felt a nagging pressure to make a decision about his educational path. In the state of Georgia, four-year-olds qualify for lottery-funded pre-K programs, and if I was going to apply for him to attend, I had to act quickly or be left out. Since Sam was our first child, I had little reference to guide me in this heart-wrenching decision: Should I attempt to homeschool, or should I send him through the system of public education?

Truth be told, I wasn't ready to commit to either path. Hadn't I just given birth to him? Yet I felt this great pressure (perhaps self-imposed) to make a decision.

So I prayed. I prayed because I didn't know what else to do. And I wanted peace.

After a few days of sweating it out, I decided to go ahead and apply for the free pre-K program that was being offered at our local high school. The teenagers at that school who were interested in pursuing early childhood education would be assistants in this program. It seemed like a good deal all around.

That school year was a success, with few complaints from either Sam or his teachers. Sam "graduated" from the program, so he was officially primed and ready for life in public elementary school the following fall. The only problem was that I wasn't ready for him to go that route. The same nagging decision revisited me: public school or homeschool? Private school was not even a consideration because of our limited finances coupled with our lack of experience in dealing with it.

So I prayed—fervently—for God to show me the path for our son. This time I felt tugged toward homeschooling. The problem was that I knew absolutely nothing about the homeschool world.

My first step in my quest for homeschool knowledge was to inquire of our local parish's educational staff. Our director of religious education, "Miss Linda," knew the parents of her students well, so she was able to steer me toward the homeschooling families for information, support, and encouragement. In no time I was pointed toward a style of homeschooling known as classical education.

The plan sounded beautiful to me. My child would read fine literature and develop an eye for Renaissance art. He might be proficient in Latin before the age of ten! Plus, we would integrate religion with academics throughout our homeschool day. Yes, this was definitely the way to go.

The Outsider | *Greg*

I've always thought homeschooling was a great idea. We have many friends who have had success with it.

But it was a brand-new thing for us. Removing our child from the public school system was an intimidating idea. If we lived close to an affordable Catholic school, we probably would not have considered homeschooling.

Neither Jennifer nor I ever wanted to be teachers, and since I had a full-time job I knew that, no matter what we decided, the responsibility would be fully on her shoulders. If things went well, I'd need to give her proper credit. But what if things didn't go so well? Would I then blame my wife?

I'd been married long enough to know that the answer to that question had to be no.

In the end we felt that to give our children an education that was not only academically sound but faithful to the Church, we'd have to do something drastic.

And the most important role I could play would be that of the supportive spouse, no matter the outcome.

Discovering the Spectrum | *Jennifer*

The second homeschool year didn't bring the same feelings of success as the first year did. The honeymoon period was clearly over. Sam, who was six at the time, started throwing terrible tantrums during his lessons, which would bring schooling to a screeching halt. Each day brought new troubles and more setbacks. We were soon miserable with one another, and homeschooling seemed to be the sole reason for our misery.

I distinctly remember thinking that I just wanted to be his mom again and no longer take on this challenging role of being his teacher. We were fighting more than loving. I couldn't understand why everything was falling apart.

Seeing us struggle through the first-grade curriculum, my parents recommended we get Sam evaluated by a mutual friend who worked as a public-school psychologist. I was shocked when our son tested "remedial" in several academic areas. As a homeschooling mom, I took those results personally. If Sam didn't learn, it was because I failed to teach him adequately. With results like that, I must be unfit for homeschooling.

To make matters even more discouraging, the psychologist asked if we ever had our child tested for Asperger's. I didn't even know what that was. The psychologist had us fill out a questionnaire. After she tallied the results, she suggested we schedule Sam for a more in-depth evaluation.

We signed Sam up right away for the evaluation but had to endure months on a waiting list. He was finally evaluated, and the results confirmed the initial suspicions of the school psychologist: Sam was diagnosed with high-functioning autism. I was told that educating him would present many challenges. The official recommendation was to discontinue homeschooling and enroll him in a public or private school. The thought was that this would give him the best environment in which to learn.

While I was being educated in the world of autism, my attention was drawn to our third son, Ben. Once I knew what to look for, I started seeing similar autistic behaviors in him, only at a much earlier age. As a precaution, we scheduled Ben to be evaluated about a month after his older brother. He came back with a slightly different diagnosis of high-functioning autism. Ben's classification was high-functioning under the classic autism spectrum, whereas Sam's fell under the category of "not otherwise specified pervasive development disorder" (NOS-PDD).

With homeschooling no longer an option, my life as a public-school parent began. Much to my surprise, things started to look up. Sam's grades quickly soared, and real learning was happening despite his diagnosis of autism. This positive turnaround told me that apparently I was never meant to homeschool. Public school really was the best. Or so I thought.

As our children progressed through the public school system, we started noticing problems with Sam and Ben. They were both struggling more than their respective classmates. Sam experienced anxiety over being in a classroom with such "bad children" that he couldn't concentrate, and he hated hearing his teacher scream. Ben couldn't cope with the unruly children in his classroom either. He withdrew into his little cocoon, pacifying himself with frequent thumb sucking.

It turned out that the elementary school the boys were attending was in the middle of a significant demographic shift. There was a major influx of new students who were undisciplined. Teacher morale was down, and many resorted to yelling at their students in a desperate attempt to regain control.

I started getting that nagging feeling again. I heard ever so faintly, as though it were a whisper in my ear, "homeschool." I quickly buried that thought.

We stuck it our for another year at the public school. Then I revisited our educational options while asking our Lord to open the right doors for us. Should we drive to an expensive and distant Catholic school? Should I go against the professional advice I had been given and homeschool? Should we look into a special-needs provision and try to transfer our children to the better public schools in the county?

We explored every option. The Catholic-school pursuits failed. Public-school transfer pursuits failed. And in our opinion, our kids' assigned public school was failing us. The only door that remained wide open and waiting for us was that homeschool door.

But, Lord, I failed as a homeschool teacher, remember?

How can I go back?

We are raising five children and hosting a radio show. This is the worst time in my life to try homeschooling! The worst!

During the last week of the summer break in 2010, I decided to give homeschooling a second attempt. I took a deep breath, marched up to the county's school board, and asked for withdrawal paperwork for all four of our boys. When the process was complete, I felt ready to tackle a new adventure of homeschooling our boys with our toddler daughter running around to make life interesting.

Homeschool Naysayers | *Greg*

When we initially tried homeschooling, one of my brothers was adamantly opposed to it. He and I had gone through the same Catholic and public schools, and we turned out OK. The homeschool kid down the street from him was "weird." After our dismal first attempt at homeschooling, we suspected that he and other friends and family members would be less than supportive of this new attempt.

But no matter what the situation, we must keep in mind that "since parents have given children their life, they are bound by the most serious obligation to educate their offspring and therefore must be recognized as the primary and principal educators."[13]

That means we are morally obligated to do whatever it takes to make sure they receive an education that will allow them to grow into faithful, educated citizens.

---

13. *Gravissimum Educationis* (Declaration on Christian Education), 3.

There is more than one way to educate a child. You might choose homeschool, private school, or public school. Each way has its challenges, and success is possible with each.

Multiple Paths for Success | *Jennifer*

As a well-meaning parent, I still succumb to anxiety over proper education for our children. However, the more I develop my relationship with Jesus and the more I draw from his love and peace to aid me through any trial in my life, the smaller my obstacles become. So I think the first step in providing a solid educational path for my children is for me to know and depend on my faith.

When I look back on what my faith in Jesus has taught me, I see time and time again how leaning on him during any trial has always been the answer. Receiving Jesus in the Eucharist, spending time with him through the beautiful tradition of eucharistic adoration, frequenting the sacrament of reconciliation, spending time with Scripture both during and outside of Mass, reaching out for support and encouragement from my brothers and sisters in Christ, educating myself on the lives of the saints, being faithful and obedient to Christ—all are opportunities that the good Lord provides to make my life spiritually successful. And they have helped me obtain guidance in educating our children.

The next step in providing the right educational path for your children is to simply know each child and know your available educational options. The ultimate goal is to unleash the learning potential for each child, and any one of the three main educational avenues— homeschool, public school, private school—could lead to that outcome.

I do believe that if homeschooling is a possibility for your family, it's worth exploring. There are too many stories of successful homeschooling to ignore. Bl. Pope John Paul II said in his apostolic exhortation *Familiaris Consortio* that "the right and duty of parents to give education is essential, since it is connected with the transmission of human life; it is original and primary with regard to the educational role of others, on account of the uniqueness of the loving relationship between parents and children; and it is irreplaceable and inalienable, and therefore incapable of being entirely delegated to others or usurped by others."[14] Imagine the potential if parents make it a priority to cooperate with God's call to be these educators.

Even if you are not in a position to homeschool, any words of wisdom you give your child will make a powerful impression. I truly believe that you can still claim that role of schooling even if your children attend a brick-and-mortar school, provided you "get in their business" and be there for them in their academic pursuits.

When our boys attended the local public elementary school, I attended a parent-teacher conference for our third son, Ben, who was then in kindergarten. His teacher told me a very touching story.

One morning Ben felt compelled to ask her about her husband. I believe he was just curious about the kind of man he was. Ben's teacher very sadly looked down and explained that her husband had passed away. Ben pondered that for a moment and then offered to pray for her. Seeing such an open display of God's love in such a public place made an impression on the teacher. This was proof to me that God can indeed be in public schools through the hearts of our informed children.

---

14. John Paul II, *Familiaris Consortio*, 36.

At the end of the day, you have to do what's right for your child and for your family. If a Catholic school is within your economic means, and your child's spiritual and academic development flourishes there, then that option is right for you. If homeschooling fits within your family dynamic and budget, and your child flourishes there, then that option is right. If the local public school is all you have, and your child flourishes there, then that's the right educational choice for your child.

However, if learning is being curtailed in any of these environments, do not be afraid to change for the benefit of your child. Some families I've talked to have explored all three roads before settling on the right educational path.

Some educational options are not available to everyone. That's fine. You will be fine. Your child will be fine. Stay close to Jesus and lean on him during good times and bad, and you will be on the right path.

Educating your child should never be downplayed as just something kids have to go through. No matter which method you ultimately decide for your child, remember, God exists there, too. He's in the homeschool with you whenever you invite him to be a part of your learning. And he accompanies your child to the school building through your intercessory prayers and in their precious little hearts.

If you continue to lean on God in matters such as these and quite honestly do your best, God will see you through. He will show you what's truly important for your child. The answer may not come overnight, and it might even take years for clarity to be yours, but the answer will come in God's time.

In But Not of
Our Tech-Savvy World

"Yes, there are dangers with technology. But
with responsibility and a spiritual focus, it's nothing
short of amazing what we as Catholics can create and
learn about our faith through the latest
and greatest of technological advancements."

chapter twelve
HERE WE ARE NOW; ENTERTAIN US

Define "Good" Entertainment | *Jennifer*

I believe work is both good for the body and good for the soul. Over the years I have come to derive much satisfaction from a productive day of maintaining our busy household while working in our ministry. But too much work, without enough rest and recreation to maintain proper balance, is detrimental. At some point we have to enjoy some R&R if we want to avoid burnout.

If you are on a tight budget, luxury vacations and even babysitters are not always possible. You need some Band-Aid solutions for R&R when getting away is just not a possibility. A movie or novel can give me the relief that I'm looking for. I get to mentally transport myself into a different reality.

Of course, entertainment is good for the body and good for the soul, provided that it is actually "good" to begin with. Not only can good entertainment lift your spirit, inspire you to challenge your fears, or console an emotional hurt, but it can also draw you closer to our Lord.

The problem is that we don't always seek out this type of entertainment. And to make matters worse, we can easily redefine *immoral* entertainment as *good* entertainment. Thus we delude ourselves into thinking we're doing nothing wrong. The wrong kinds of entertainment can darken your spirit, negatively influence your ideas on morals, and draw you toward the evil one.

So what's *good* entertainment? I can only tell you that my definition of "good" has surely matured along with the rest of me. There was a time when my version of good was not very good at all.

Before I became a mother, I had a highly secular approach to entertainment. For some reason it never occurred to me to allow my Christian faith to influence the kind of entertainment I consumed. As long as I perceived myself to be a Catholic in good standing, what did it matter what entertainment I pursued on any given night?

Whenever Greg and I went out on a date, we inevitably wound up seeing the latest movie. This was our favorite pastime when we were a newly married couple. Movie ratings and moral content never factored into our decision-making when it came time to pick the film. What did matter to us was only our level of interest in seeing it.

The same could be said about the music we listened to, the television shows we watched, and the books we read. If it was funny or interesting, we'd entertain our minds with it. God was not part of this equation, and we didn't think he had to be.

Sadly, this attitude toward entertainment followed me right into our parenting years. After twelve to fourteen hours of being a stay-at-home mom with high-energy boys, the idea of relaxing in front of the TV was more than appealing. Snuggling up against Greg with a large bowl of popcorn was my well-deserved reward for any long day.

This erroneous mind-set, coupled with exhaustion, left me open to the media's oftentimes anti-Christian message. Much of the entertainment I consumed promoted moral relativism and immoral sexuality and accepted gratuitous violence. Yet I couldn't *see* the problem. Overly confident in my self-perceived holiness, I figured that whatever entertainment I liked was harmless.

Our beloved Bl. Pope John Paul II knew the influence of media. He once stated that "the film industry has become a universal medium exercising a profound influence on the development of people's attitudes and choices, and possessing a remarkable ability to influence public opinion and culture across all social and political frontiers."[15]

Not so Happy Days | *Greg*

As a dad of four boys and as a man in today's society, I have to say that, without a doubt, one of my top five pet peeves is pornography.

I hate it. It drives me absolutely nuts.

And I'm not just talking about the way pornography degrades men and women by turning them into nothing more than objects but also the culture that pornography has helped to create.

It drives me crazy when we go on a family road trip and see one billboard after another advertising "Adult Videos, Naked Waitresses, and More!" How am I supposed to explain those kinds of things to my children? And why should I have to deal with the reality that stuff like this will be shoved in their faces on a public highway?

The truth of the matter is that this problem is not new to parents of my generation. But I do believe that our generation has some particular challenges in dealing with it.

It was in our generation—those of us who grew up in the 1970s and 1980s—that a more permissive view of sexual licentiousness and other vices made their way into our living rooms, oftentimes in plain sight and at other times in the most innocent disguises

For example, a few years ago ABC television aired a two-hour *Happy Days* reunion. *Happy Days* was one of my favorite shows in the late seventies and early eighties, and I daresay I've seen just about every episode at least once.

---

15. John Paul II, address to the Plenary Assembly of the Pontifical Commission for Social Communications, March 17, 1995.

But one scene on the reunion special really jumped out at me. It was from an episode in which Fonzie was teaching his friends how to unhook a woman's bra. I distinctly remember seeing that when I was younger, and I distinctly remember thinking it was funny. But when I saw that scene again, it made me angry. I felt as though I had been tricked. Even thirty years ago television was sneakily teaching me evil things in innocent packages.

After all, *Happy Days* was a show about the innocence of the 1950s. It was a family show. But it was also a show where the cool guy was the one who was the antithesis of monogamy. And this show, when I wasn't even a teenager, taught me that if I wanted to be cool, I should be able to unhook a bra as did the Fonz.

In recent years I've noticed a lot of old television shows being repackaged and sold as DVD box collections. At first I thought this was a great idea, but on closer inspection, even these nostalgic television shows require me to approach them with much suspicion.

One such set (and I'm embarrassed to admit I own it) are the two 1980s science-fiction miniseries called *V,* about an alien invasion. When I decided to rewatch the second *V* miniseries, my fond memories of watching that show as a kid were spoiled. With adult eyes I saw the ideologies involving abortion and lack of respect for Roman Catholic clergy being forced on me. Whereas I once looked at that series as a campy romp in B-grade science fiction, I now noticed scenes in which the filmmakers were trying to force their views on a built-in audience.

What does this kind of stuff do to us? If we look at the path that entertainment has taken since the 1970s, we can see direct evidence of doors opening to images that are more and more graphic and immoral.

Brian Gail, the author of *Fatherless* (which is one of the most incredible Catholic novels I've ever read), made an insightful observation about the moral decline in entertainment, describing it as a direct result of the invasion of cable television in the 1980s. In an interview with the *National Catholic Register,* he said:

> My generation failed the Church, the country and ourselves. Now we're failing the next generation. Enough already. We simply decided not to trust our children with the truth. As a consequence they are making decisions absent any objective moral reason. They are stumbling into terrible pain and suffering which will have a ruinous half-life.[16]

At the risk of more hand-wringing, let me say this: As someone who grew up in the shadow of cable television, has worked in the Internet world, and has had a direct impact on modern-day Catholic new media, I can relate to Gail's words in more ways than one.

What Are You Hiding? | *Jennifer*
I probably remained ignorant about entertainment and its effects for so long because I wanted to enjoy myself after a long day with the kids. But this could not go on forever. As time went on, our growing children were taking a greater interest in the way we as a family valued entertainment. Suddenly there were more sets of eyes watching TV and movies with us. Well, God, in his infinite mercy, got my attention before things got out of hand. How did he do it? He sent me a letter. Well, not exactly a letter, more like a pamphlet.

---

16. Brian Gail, quoted by Tim Drake in "American Downfall, Fictionalized," *National Catholic Register,* April 7, 2010.

I attended an ecumenical meeting at my local parish and came home with a goody bag filled with religious flyers and booklets. On pouring out the contents of that bag onto my bed, I noticed a rather small but intriguing black-and-white pamphlet sticking out of the pile. Its simple story and stick-figure art challenged me to take a second look at the moral content of media in my home.

The pamphlet asked me to meditate on this: If I were to invite Jesus into my home right now and let him peruse all of the content of my closets, drawers, storage boxes, and so on, would I have anything to be ashamed of in there? That simple question hit me like a ton of bricks.

I had some major cleaning up to do. Like Adam and Eve in the Garden of Eden feeling shame at the sudden realization of their nakedness, I felt a similar shame over how casual I had been with the entertainment I chose to consume.

I discussed this new insight with Greg, and we decided to do some moral house cleaning. We sorted through all of the entertainment media in our house and got rid of anything that had questionable moral content in it. We didn't give things away or try to recoup some of the money we'd spent on them by reselling but actually tossed them into the trash can outside our house. Out went many books from Oprah's book club. Out went music containing explicit lyrics. Out went gratuitously violent movies and overly graphic novels. And with that, out went the old mind-set of casual acceptance of any entertainment without regard to its moral shortcomings.

I Was a Pop-Culture Glutton | *Greg*

After we tossed out the entertainment garbage we had in our house, something interesting happened. I found I could breathe again. I knew that our life was more in alignment with the will of God, which led to new freedom. Detaching myself from anything that takes my focus away from others and away from God leads to true and genuine freedom.

Somehow I'd adopted the thinking that I was obligated to keep up with the latest movies, the most popular television shows, whatever the entertainment world told me to watch. When a movie won an Academy Award, I felt an obligation to see that movie, even if it was a stinking pile of rubbish.

Just to emphasize how pathetic this obsession was, let me admit yet one more embarrassing thing about my past.

Jennifer and I met after we both auditioned for a play in college. At that time in my life I was bored out of my mind and constantly looking for something to fill the gaps that seemed to occupy my every day. That's one of the reasons someone like me, who'd never been in a theatrical production, ended up auditioning for (and receiving) the lead role in a play.

But I still had time on my hands. And without a serious path in life, I escaped several times a week to a local movie theater. This was right before Christmas, a major time when new movies are released. Out of a combination of sheer boredom and this weird sense of pop-culture loyalty, I would go to a theater and see a movie literally several days in a row.

After a couple of weeks, I had seen every single movie showing in any theater within twenty miles of where I lived.

My friend, look up the word *loser* in your dictionary and you'll see a picture of me when I was twenty-four years old.

Even today I struggle with the strange need to be aware of all the movies and television shows waiting just around the corner.

While I have no plans to stop watching television or movies completely, I have become aware of the addictive nature of it all. I must constantly work at moderation and ask God for help in this area.

St. Paul tells us, "For freedom Christ has set us free; stand fast, therefore, and do not submit again to a yoke of slavery" (Galatians 5:1). St. Paul's use of the word *free* was in relation to the covenant relationship of Abraham and his children, one of whom was born into slavery and the other free (see Galatians 4:21–24). But the statement can also apply to all things that can take control of our lives and remove our God-given freedoms.

Entertainment can be a gift, but as with many attractive things in life, it doesn't take much for us to become enslaved by it. Paul says, "For you were called to freedom, brethren; Only do not use your freedom as an opportunity for the flesh, but through love be servants of one another" (Galatians 5:13).

Eye Candy for Kids | *Jennifer*

Once Greg and I started to share a desire to avoid morally objectionable material in our entertainment, guiding our children's consumption of entertainment would be smooth sailing. Well, yes and no.

I was gullible enough to believe that moderating children's stations like PBS, Disney, and Nick Jr. was unnecessary. The bubbly and colorful nature of their programming made it difficult for me to see the small and innocent ways morals were being loosened and distorted. Lies were served in bite-sized nuggets. While I believe there are some safe programs designed for kids out there, the climate remains far from one that would allow me to be worry-free.

Once I knew what to look for, it became easier for me to identify and avoid programs on behalf of my children.

In today's world of multiple sources of entertainment delivery, the worry does not end with clamping down on our television sets. The convenience of video streaming, for example, necessitates vigilance. Certain on-demand video streaming services have navigational menus that are not family-friendly. I made the mistake of allowing one of our sons to choose a cartoon to watch through our Netflix account, and while he was searching for the children's category he surfed by the horror genre, where he was unexpectedly subjected to glimpses of graphic movie posters featuring all levels of gore and scantily clad women. I won't make that mistake again.

The simple truth is that, if you have children in your home and you love media entertainment, it won't take long for your kids to love it too. You can have a positive and safe experience with this kind of entertainment, provided that you remain vigilant in knowing what they are watching and limiting their exposure, depending on their age. The website for the American Academy of Pediatrics has plenty of guidelines to help you gain some perspective on how much is too much TV for your kids. We've gone through seasons when we've limited TV entertainment to Fridays and Saturdays, leaving us free to focus more on family responsibilities, reading, and playing outdoors.

Stay informed! If your kids are watching a show you've never heard of (and that, frankly, you have no interest or time to watch yourself), do a Google search for parent reviews on that show's exact title. Then decide, is this a show you want your kids to see?

Be prepared to follow through with all your parental enforcements. It's a tough job but well worth the investment of your time.

Help Is Out There | *Greg*
Read movie reviews. Some of our favorite movie-review websites

include catholicnews.com/movies at Catholic News Service, which provides reviews from a moral perspective. Another is decentfilms. com, which is run by Catholic film critic Steven Greydanus. And one non-Catholic website we frequent to help us review not only movies but television, websites, and video games is www.commonsense-media.org.

Program your television to work for you. If you're a television enthusiast like me, then take the time to learn your television's parental controls. Most televisions and cable systems from the past ten years offer you options to hide or block certain channels, even removing them from any on-screen television guides. It is our hope that our kids will never know MTV exists. While that's unrealistic, hiding that channel from our satellite system's viewing guide, along with any other channels with inappropriate content, will go a long way toward helping our children be more judicious in their viewing.

If you don't have the time or ability to customize your channel lineup, research the current parental-control options that are available online and find the best solution based on the equipment you have.

Avoid commercials whenever possible. Between women mud-wrestling in beer commercials during a football game and contraception commercials between building shows on HGTV, we constantly have to fight the marketing machine that threatens to deaden our senses about immoral living.

Limit the number of television sets in the house. One or two televisions is really enough for even the largest of families. Keeping all televisions in public areas of the home makes them far easier to moderate. While many parents think nothing of providing their kids of high-school age and younger with television sets of their own, having a television in a bedroom is generally a bad idea. Encourage your kids to treat their brains to a good book instead and to enjoy a better sleep.

Talk to your children about the rights and wrongs of entertainment. Point out to your kids the problems you encounter with entertainment. Use such moments as opportunities to explain Catholic teachings. Let them know why you can't condone or support media content that includes objectionable material.

While it would be tempting to keep our kids in a Catholic bubble for as long as they'll let us, we'll do them and the world a greater service by encouraging them to discern right from wrong. They can then be lights in this world of darkness by the time they leave the family nest.

chapter thirteen

GOOD NEWS FOR TECHIES

We've Gone Wireless | *Greg*

Jennifer and I were both born in 1970. It is said that ours is the last analog generation. We are the last who will remember life before cellphones, the Internet, and cable and satellite television services reached the far ends of the world and our living room sofas.

It was in our youth that Pong took the honor of being the first home video-game system. And since then we've gone from Pong to Pac-Man to Atari to Nintendo to XBox 360 to games that recognize full-body movement via infrared motion bars. We've gone from programming bit-mapped squares on Timex Sinclairs and Commodore Vic 20s to surfing the Internet on smartphones anywhere in the world. It's impossible to imagine what our children will see in their lifetimes and how technology will impact the way they live.

It's safe to suppose that technologies will only continue to evolve. (I'm still waiting for an affordable, consumer-level jetpack so I can fly to the store when we run out of coffee.) So we must also ask ourselves, is all of this technology a good thing? Or perhaps we should be asking, is there a way to use all this technology for a greater purpose?

I'm not criticizing technology. I'm the first to admit that I'm a borderline technology addict. In our house alone we have six computers, two smartphones, two iPads, and three gaming systems (but only one television).

But are all these things just toys? Or are they tools that can help shape my faith?

Jennifer and I have been loyal fans of just about everything Apple creates. We would always find a way to purchase the latest and greatest gadget that promised to make our lives easier. We had LED screens in multiple sizes throughout the house. Sure, we could justify having them because of our work, but let's be real. They provided access to hundreds of exciting games and movies and enabled us to make silly family photos. There was something for every member of the family, no matter the person's age or level of geekiness.

But something felt wrong with this picture. It was as if our family was slowly being turned into a combination of techno zombies and couch potatoes. Tempers became short. The kids resorted to arguing rather than discussing their differences. Meals were skipped because remaining seated in front of the computer was more important than eating. The kids struggled to use their own imaginations; it was easier for them to receive information electronically than to produce ideas with their own minds.

The more Jennifer and I grew in our spirituality, the more we began to see what would happen if we didn't make some changes in the way we used all these electronic devices.

If It's Good Enough for the Pope | *Jennifer*

While using too much technology has the potential to derail us from what really matters in our walk toward Christ, using it creatively can help us toward our faith-filled goals.

In his message for the 44th World Day of Social Communications, Pope Benedict XVI wrote in regard to priests, "They will best achieve this aim [of using technology] if they learn, from the time of their formation, how to use these technologies in a competent and appropriate way, shaped by sound theological insights and reflecting a strong priestly spirituality grounded in constant dialogue with the Lord."

In many ways this message applies to laypeople as well. The Holy Father continued: "The increased availability of the new technologies demands greater responsibility on the part of those called to proclaim the Word, but it also requires them to become more focused, efficient and compelling in their efforts." [17]

That's what a lot of this really boils down to. Yes, there are dangers with technology. But with responsibility and a spiritual focus, it's nothing short of amazing what we as Catholics can create and learn about our faith through the latest and greatest of technological advancements.

Technological Temperance | *Greg*

Whether we like to admit it or not, technology impacts all of the subjects we've discussed in this book—marriage, parenting, understanding the sacraments, living out our faith. With proper thinking and direction, we can learn how to use this technology to better understand and grow in our faith and also help other people to do the same. On the other hand, abuse of the same technology—spending too much of our time with web surfing, for example—can make us falter in our faith. It can drag us into slothlike behavior and trap us in pornography, among other things.

As with many aspects of our consumerist world, our society is in desperate need of moderation when it comes to technology. When I

---

17. Benedict VXI, "World Day of Social Communications," Regina Caeli address, May 16, 2010.

see thousands of people waiting in line to get their hands on the latest and greatest new gadget, I can't help but think that we could all use some technological temperance.

Temperance, which the *Cathechism of the Catholic Church* describes as "the moral virtue that moderates the attraction of pleasures and provides balance in the use of created goods" (CCC, 1809), ensures that we keep our desires within the limits of what is honorable.

The challenge is to learn how to balance the technological advantages of today's culture with a genuine freedom from attachment to material possessions. Just as a person on a diet learns to balance calories, we must learn to balance the amount of time we spend using technology and the influence we allow it to have over our thoughts and behavior.

New Media Evangelization | *Jennifer*

In 2005 most people had not yet heard of podcasts (MP3 audio files created on a computer or other recording device and made freely available on the Internet via download). As an experiment, Greg decided to create one of these for our Rosary Army apostolate. He saw it as a fun and creative way to update people on the latest news regarding our nonprofit.

Interestingly enough, while the early podcasts quickly gained a listenership because of our built-in online audience of worldwide Rosary Army volunteers, it wasn't until Greg was laid off from his job a couple of months later that the podcast really came to life. Initially (and you can still download and hear these recordings yourself from our website, www.RosaryArmy.com), each episode focused primarily on business issues related to Rosary Army itself. But soon things would turn highly personal.

One evening after Greg lost his job, he took a chance and vented his emotions into his recording iPod. Instead of talking just about Rosary Army, he shared something infinitely more personal—his pain over his unexpected job loss. With a few simple clicks, he uploaded his emotional show and went back to the business of finding a new job.

To our amazement, e-mails started flooding in from around the globe.

"You have no idea how much I could relate to your situation," a listener wrote.

"It was like I was listening to myself," another stated.

And there it was: a connection between souls via MP3 players and computers, of all things.

Within a few weeks I joined Greg in producing the podcast. Together we shared the joys and struggles of Catholic parenting and marriage from a personal perspective. When something happened to us, good or bad, we did our best to share the honest feelings that we were experiencing—even if our reactions weren't the best or most Catholic of reactions.

To us this is the single most important thing Catholics need to realize about technology: If we use it to connect with others, to help people in their lives, to help us be companions in each other's journeys to a life in Christ, then technology is a tool for the conversion of souls.

Behind the Curve | *Greg*

Eventually the Rosary Army Catholic Podcast ended up winning the 2006 Award for Best General Podcast—from the People's Choice Podcast Awards, which are intended primarily for secular media. This proved to us that Catholic media can not only "preach to the choir" but also reach a secular audience in a way that is open and honest and welcoming. It proved that people want positive content.

I am absolutely convinced that if we as Catholics start making content that artistically matches or exceeds content developed by secular producers, the world will welcome this.

This idea is so exciting to me that it's basically become my life and livelihood.

In 2007, I left my career of more than a decade in the IT industry to work full-time as a Catholic new-media missionary. Jennifer and I have created podcasts and videos (seen at www.ThatCatholicShow .com) and helped start a new-media ministry (www.SQPN.com). The annual Catholic New Media Conference (www.CNMC.SQPN) that we helped to start continues to bring together other media missionaries every year. We eventually were hired to host a daily three-hour talk show on SiriusXM satellite radio, and most recently we've started an apostolate called New Evangelizers (www.NewEvangelizers.com). I'm not suggesting that all Catholics quit their well-paying jobs to do the same. But I do believe that every single one of us has an important role to fill in this arena of new media.

And I'm not alone in believing this.

The pope has an iPad. In fact, in 2011 he used it to launch a Vatican news portal (http://news.va). He also has two early-model iPods. Our Holy Father gets it: The Catholic Church can use the latest technologies for our own faith development as well as for effectively sharing our faith.

In 2005 there were *maybe* twenty-five to fifty Catholic podcasts available online. Now there are hundreds; soon there will be thousands.

In 2007 there were *maybe* five Catholic applications available on smartphones. That number has increased exponentially.

We're still years behind our secular and Protestant friends in terms of resources being invested in this important work for the Church.

And that's something we can and should try to fix.

In a speech at the fall 2010 meeting of the United States Conference of Catholic Bishops, Bishop Ronald Herzog, a member of the USCCB communications committee, said of teens and technology:

> The news, entertainment, [teens'] friends—are all coming to them through their mobile devices and through their social networks.... If the Church is not on their mobile device, it doesn't exist. The Church does not have to change its teaching to reach young people, but we must deliver it to them in a new way.[18]

That statement should shake us to the core!

Our world is evolving at a rate that is difficult to keep up with, and rapidly changing technologies are at the heart of that evolution. Bishop Herzog is correct in saying that we need to rapidly embrace and develop new ways to deliver the timeless message of the Church.

As it stands, we Catholics have done a terrible job of sharing information. I'm not suggesting that everyone needs to start building websites and mobile apps. If you're not tech-savvy, that's fine. But if you have an e-mail account, a social-networking profile, or an iPod, you can be part of the New Evangelization through these media.

If you have a favorite Catholic website, then tell your friends about it. If you listen to Catholic podcasts, encourage your family to listen to them as well. And just as important, if you're able, financially support those who create this content. Sadly, a major reason why Catholics are so far behind in this area is that too few are willing to open their

---

18. "Bishops Seeking Missionaries for Digital Continent," *Zenit*, November 16, 2010.

wallets to help support those who can and want to develop this type of catechesis.

The good news is that when we all start to actively support Catholic creators and organizations who produce and develop podcasts, blogs, and other new media, we're going to see incredible evangelization in action. And we'll also assure that future generations will not disappear from the Church but instead become her most active evangelists.

The reality is that the Catholic Church has a long history of leading the way when it comes to advancements in society. The Church established the first hospitals and schools. Vatican Radio was established in 1931, and *Life Is Worth Living*, Servant of God Fulton Sheen's prime-time television show on NBC in the 1950s, won the good bishop an Emmy Award for Most Outstanding Television Personality. The great St. Maximilian Kolbe also "got it": He published a monthly review, *Knight of the Immaculata*, in order to "illuminate the truth and show the true way to happiness." Its circulation grew from five thousand to seventy thousand in just five years.[19]

If we all start sharing what's available and supporting talented developers who want to make even more, the Catholic Church can be the brightest light in all of cyberspace. We're blessed to play a part in what could be one of the most exciting moments in all of history in terms of opportunities for evangelization.

Look at it this way. We recorded our early podcasts in a recording studio we set up in our closet. Those free programs have since been downloaded nearly four million times. That's technology. That's evangelization. And that's nothing compared to what we're capable of when we work together.

---

19. "Maximilian Kolbe: Priest hero of a death camp," www.catholic-pages.com.

conclusion

While we are all imperfect in our own ways, our flaws should never cause us to abandon our duty to love our neighbor. Instead we should consider our imperfections to be opportunities to seek God even more. God faithfully waits for us to journey toward him. And through the sacraments and the quiet whisperings of the Holy Spirit, we can live out this journey with great hope.

But this journey is not just for you and me. It's for our parents, spouses, kids, coworkers, friends, enemies, and even that lady wearing the big hat in the front pew at Mass. The journey toward God is for humanity.

Our faith in Jesus Christ should be embedded in every action we take throughout the day—twenty-four hours a day and seven days a week. This holds true whether you are a cradle Catholic or a convert. Are you deciding how to educate children, live out a good marriage, approach technology and entertainment? Every decision in life should be made with the guidance of our faith in Christ.

"The way of Christ 'leads to life'; a contrary way 'leads to destruction'" (*CCC*, 1696, referencing Matthew 7:13 and Deuteronomy 30:15–20).

What does it mean to be one of the Catholics next door in today's world? It means to struggle. It means to fail. It means to forgive and to seek forgiveness and accept it when it is given. It means to be guardians of our minds and hearts and to help others do the same.

We may be stupid Catholics from time to time. We're all under spiritual construction, perpetual works in progress. Let us all continually progress toward the Lord and his kingdom.

As Steve Jobs was so well known for saying, *there's one more thing.*

It's now just a few months since we completed the initial drafts of this book. The manuscript has gone through discussions, editing, changes to the cover, more editing, a few more cover changes, and Jennifer and I even recorded this whole thing as an audiobook.

At home, our busy days as parents have continued, unending, constantly changing. We work and laugh and cry, fret, and laugh again.

Life keeps happening, as life is wont to do, and we've found ourselves continually pulled back to the chapters in this book and are drawn by the intensity of how some of these chapters resonate so loudly even in our own lives. By our need to be filled by God. To understand his will in our lives. To immerse ourselves in his grace so as to handle the daily roadblocks of life that never seem to end.

We look back at some of the advice we've given within these pages and ask ourselves, "Are we walking the walk of this talk we've been talking?"

One of the most difficult, soul-searching, honesty-requiring chapters of this book for us to write was about being open to life, being open to the exhaustion of late-night feedings, more years of whining toddlerhood, and more decades of worry about the safety of yet another child growing into adulthood in this world of oftentimes questionable security. Are we really up to the trials of being fruitful and multiplying, with all the baggage that accompanies that journey?

This is an area in which, as parents, we're constantly in flux and regularly tested. And this past year has been particularly challenging for us.

Because of our busy lives, hosting three hours of talk radio each day, and juggling our schedules and that of five children, combined with our needs to pray, play, rest, and recoup and added to that, the financial challenges and the mornings when we're certain we're the worst parents ever we sometimes can't see clearly the blessings God is waiting to give us.

In the past year we've had conversations (so countless we won't even try to recall them) about our physical, mental, and spiritual inability to properly care for an additional child. We're so busy. We were writing a book and have other possible book projects on the way. We started a new apostolate (NewEvangelizers.com). We still have full-time jobs. Our pay at work was frozen because of budget constraints and we can't afford another child. We don't even have room in our house to put another bed!

And most important, our other children desperately need more of us right now.

But are any of these valid excuses for not doing the will of God?

Again, being open to life does not mean having as many children as physically possible, and openness to life is not actually the core of what I'm talking about right here.

Are we following the will of God in all areas of our lives?

For us this year, that question centered particularly around the number of children we have or will have. But it also affected other areas of our lives. This year, the question of following God's will has meant being open to the possibility of what God wants for our family. To answer that question, we decided to lessen the periods of abstinence each month during Jennifer's fertile cycle, and we trusted God a little more. We didn't really want another baby right now, but if God sent one our way, we'd be open to it.

And he did.

One morning this past September, I was trying to get a few extra minutes of sleep when I felt Jennifer reach for me. Thinking she just wanted to hold hands in the darkness before the children woke up and our day began at a thousand miles an hour, as it normally does, I instead felt a hard piece of plastic being slipped between my fingers.

In the darkness, I immediately knew what Jennifer was trying to tell me. I bolted upright, turned on the light, and looked at the pregnancy test in my hand, clearly telling me I was a dad once again.

Jennifer was pregnant.

Jennifer briefly mentioned this unplanned pregnancy earlier in the book, but it was difficult for us to adequately explain it at the time. It seems appropriate to write about it now, though, in light of the ways that God constantly pulls us closer to him through every circumstance and every single day.

On that day, we were ticked off.

I know that sounds crazy, but we were. For all the reasons listed above, this simply didn't make sense. What was God doing? Did he not see the emptiness of our checking account? Did he not know that Jennifer was going to put her head through the wall already because of the challenges of trying to homeschool our children while also hosting an international radio program every day? How in the world could we fit a baby into the mix?

We took the day off to process this information, catch our breath, and figure out our next steps. Jennifer would quit our radio show. No. Perhaps not. We'd try once more to find an acceptable private school for our children. Perhaps. We'd try for the fifth time to sell our house, knowing how pointless it would be to do so in the current economy.

Throughout the day we wrestled with God, with our thoughts, with our insecurities.

And despite the negativity we were so quick to bring to the table, the reality started to sink in.

We'd been blessed again. Jennifer was *pregnant*.

By the end of that day, I'd kissed her stomach, talked to the baby in her womb, and told him or her that I'd already fallen in love.

In the weeks that followed, we again looked into a private school, and this time God provided a miracle for us to pay for the tuition. The boys have adjusted and are thriving in ways we could never have imagined. On our radio show, we shared news of the pregnancy, and we both committed to sticking with our jobs until God revealed some other path. It would be difficult juggling a new child with everything else, but we were already thinking of names and figuring out how to rearrange the house to accommodate another little life.

Then, at a routine checkup, the ultrasound was unable to find a heartbeat. The baby was not growing. Devastation grabbed hold of us with its deep claws, and we mourned. A third miscarriage? How was this cruelty possible? Why, God? Why put us through this emotional train wreck?

At a follow-up appointment a few days later, having accepted this terrible loss, there was another miracle in our lives: a heartbeat after all.

My stomach churned in a thousand directions, the emotional spectrum of joy and worry and everything in between virtually unbearable.

Two weeks after that, again, a change. The baby had, in fact, died in the womb. A certainty this time.

The subtitle of this book, *Adventures in Imperfect Living,* isn't just a catchy phrase. All of our lives are full of adventures, and the truth is that you and I don't always handle them perfectly. Yet the fact remains that the adventures never stop, and God constantly surprises us. We thought that when we finished this book, perhaps things would be stagnant for a time, with no major challenges or changes coming our way. But that, of course, is naive.

Our lives might drastically change once again by the time this book is printed just weeks from now. Your life too has most likely changed in some way, large or small, just while reading these pages.

Our hope is that, in your own adventures of imperfect living, you'll be open to the will of God in all circumstances. That's what it really means to be the Catholics next door. To be open to living out our faith wherever we may be, with whomever we encounter, and whatever surprising challenges may be tossed our way.

We may not always see clearly the purpose for our misadventures, as was the case that morning last September when we discovered this last pregnancy. But when we hold fast to God and include him in every step of every adventurous day, purpose gains clarity and, with time, we grow in the holiness he provides

And, God willing, when all is said and done, and we've lived our last adventure, God will have led us through our hesitations, our imperfections, and our not-so-stellar days to be the perfect children he's always meant for us to be.

ABOUT THE AUTHORS

Greg and Jennifer Willits are the hosts of *The Catholics Next Door,* a daily three-hour program that can be heard on The Catholic Channel on SiriusXM. They are the founders of NewEvangelizers.com, Rosary Army, *That Catholic Show,* and several other apostolates dedicated to helping people develop a greater relationship with Jesus Christ. Married since 1995, they are the parents of five children.